BY THE SAME AUTHOR

The Kennedy Promise

The Spoiled Child of the Western World

THE PARTIES

Republicans and Democrats
in This Century

THE
PARTIES

Republicans and Democrats in This Century

HENRY FAIRLIE

St. Martin's Press New York

Copyright © 1978 by The New Republic Magazine
All rights reserved.
For information, write:
St. Martin's Press, Inc.,
175 Fifth Ave.,
New York, N.Y. 10010.
Manufactured in the United States of America
Library of Congress Catalog Card Number: 77-9176

Library of Congress Cataloging in Publication Data

Fairlie, Henry, 1924-
The parties.

1. Republican Party.   2. Democratic Party.
3. United States—Politics and government—20th century.
I. Title.
JK2261.F24   329.3   77-9176
ISBN 0-312-59738-X

Acknowledgment

I want to thank Martin Peretz, the editor, and Robert J. Myers, the publisher, of the *New Republic* for the assistance and encouragement which they have given to me in the preparation of this book, some parts of which appeared in that journal.

Contents

One: The Elephant Graveyard

Two: The Donkey Serenade

ONE

The
Elephant
Graveyard

Bleached Bones–And
Two Broken Tusks

IT TOOK SOME TIME after the election of 1976 for people to realize just how terrible a defeat the Republican party had suffered. The fairly respectable showing of Gerald Ford—although it was not all that respectable by any count, considering he was the incumbent—at first obscured the savagery of the wounds the electors had inflicted on the party as a whole. It won back only a handful of the forty-three previously safe Republican seats in Congress it had lost in the midterm elections in 1974. Out in the states, there are today three times as many Democratic as Republican governors; and the Democratic party now holds a majority in both houses of thirty-six of the state legislatures. Even in the four states where the Republicans still control both houses of the legislatures there is only one Republican governor. From the presidency, to Congress, to the governorships, to the state legislatures, the Republican party in 1976 was worse than decimated. Whether at the federal or the state level, it hardly looks like a governing party at all, let alone the "normal governing party" of the country.

Contemplating these figures after the election, Kevin Phillips, the political analyst, said that the Republican party is approaching a condition of "critical non-mass." Yet it was he who only seven years before had written a book called The *Emerging Republican Majority,* in which he said that "a new era has begun," in which Republicanism would be triumphant. The paperback edition of the book may still be found in some bookstores, with the unfortunate legend spelled across its cover: "The Political Bible of the Nixon Years." From "emerging majority" to "critical non-mass" in seven years! Politics does not move as fast as that. The analysis itself was simply askew.

It is not only Kevin Phillips who has been so astray; he may have had the misfortune to write the bible, but others were carrying the same gospel. Richard Nixon himself spoke of the "new majority" that he was putting together; the Southern Strategy was trumpeted as if it were a secret weapon; there was talk of the flight to the suburbs and the pell-mell rush to the Sun Belt; and perhaps above all it was said that the New Deal coalition was at last finally dissolving.

One could paper the walls of the White House with the volumes of tables and charts and graphs which, in the past eight years, have demonstrated, beyond sensible doubt, that the Republicans were about to replace the Democrats as the normal governing party of the nation. Not only has it not happened, but at the end of 1976 the Republican party seemed to be as far from attaining this position as forty years earlier after its first shattering defeat in 1936.

Something about the Republican party—about its very nature—has not been properly noticed in recent years. Parties have characters, and before we begin adding up the blocs of voters who must be appeased here and tempted there, we should pay attention to these characters. We should feel the weave of the parties between our thumbs and forefingers. We should be able to rub them and know their texture or, to change the image, to smell and taste them, and know their vintage. Parties have color, they have bouquet, they have flavor.

If we cannot know a party like this, it is probably no good for man or beast. This is the condition of the Republican party today, and it is Republicans themselves who are saying so. This does not mean that it will not recover in time; but its sickness now is radical, even if it is not terminal. It is not partisanship that compels one to be severe in one's judgment. It is Republicans themselves who are to-day being most harsh in their self-criticism. The simple fact is that the Republican party, in the forty-four years since it was first defeated by Franklin Roosevelt, has shed the character which it previously had, but found no other character which the majority of the people can smell, feel, taste, know, enjoy: denounce or cheer. There is no savor to it, no richness of nature. To try to give a picture of it is sometimes like attempting to breathe some animal life into a pile of bleached bones.

Nationally and in the states it was the Republican party and not only Gerald Ford that was so savaged in 1976. People vote for parties, for what they feel the parties to be, much more than the pollsters and the political scientists are able to show by their measurements. Perhaps the electors are standing more loosely in their relationship with the parties than in the past, but that does not mean that the parties do not matter to them. *The Party's Over,* said the political journalist David Broder in the title of a book he published in 1972: a rather melodramatic title, which the thesis of his book did not in fact sustain. But the truth is that the party is not over; that beyond dispute it was an advantage for Jimmy Carter in 1976 to be a Democrat, and a disadvantage for Gerald Ford to be a Republican, and that the same was true in other contests across the country.

The electors cannot, and therefore do not, judge a candidate solely on his personal qualities. "Not all the men nominated have previous political records that permit the voters to study them as individuals," wrote Al Smith. "They must take them on the faith of the party they represent." If they had acted only on their judgments of *what they knew* of Ford and Carter in 1976, the electors might well have returned a different verdict. But there was another basis for judgment: what they knew of the parties. It was not Watergate, not his pardon of Nixon, not anything that he himself had done or left undone, that was the albatross round Ford's neck; it was the fact that he was a Republican.

Even in our day and age, there is such a thing as folk memory. It operates in elections, more strongly than is dreamed of in the philosophies of many political observers. That folk memory, in all the mysterious ways in which it is transmitted, attaches itself less to individual politicians than to parties. If the main worries of many Americans in 1976, as seems generally to be agreed, were jobs and the state of the economy, then it was not from Ford but from the Republicans that they withheld their trust, not to Carter but to the Democrats that they in the end tentatively gave it. For in such a choice, the folk memory of the two parties tells: the still underlying feeling—it is hardly stronger than that—that the Republican party cannot be trusted on such things, that it has been for two generations, and still is, too much the party of "they," governing "We, the people," in the interests of "them."

At the Republican National Convention in 1976, there was one event followed by one vignette that together told it all. Speaking from his own long-ago background spent as a boy on the streets of New York City, as a Republican senator who can carry the state of New York, as a humane man who seems to feel in his bones the miseries of those less fortunate than he, Jacob Javits tried to tell the convention of the problems of the poor and the underprivileged which should be concerning it. But hardly anyone chose to listen. He was speaking of things of which they did not want to hear; and of course he was speaking also of things that would help to decide the election.

Then came the vignette, when the name of Ronald Reagan was put in nomination and his supporters brayed on their foolish trumpets. On and on went their hooting; and the television cameras caught the face of Jacob Javits among the other delegates from New York. There was on his face a smile, not of vindictiveness or even of impatience, but of a sad forgiveness for what his party was doing to itself, an almost faraway smile of unaccusing melancholy:

> Alas! regardless of their doom,
> The little victims play;
> No sense have they of ills to come,
> Nor care beyond the day.

This man whose father was a Jew, an immigrant, a janitor, and who had been brought up in a tenement on the Lower East Side: in the whole of his life, which has spanned all but the first four years of this century, he had seen so much,

14

but more than all he had seen his party again and again throw away the very people it needs.

"All the voter wants to know is, are you interested in him," said Robert Humphreys, a Republican strategist in the Eisenhower years. But to too many people in the past fifty years the Republican party has said that it is not interested in *them*: to too many who have in fact been looking, again and again, for an alternative to the Democrats as the normal governing party of the country. For a nation needs not just two parties but two *governing* parties; and the unwillingness of the people to trust the Republicans with government is to be seen, even more than at the national level, in the dominance of the Democrats today in the governors' mansions and state legislatures.

It is a national tragedy that the Republican party is so weak and so feckless; and the tragedy will be prolonged if the Republicans now exhaust themselves in a meaningless feud between its "moderate" and its "conservative" wings. All parties are coalitions, and a party with a genuine political life in itself would have no difficulty in containing both moderates and conservatives; and not only containing them, but out of their alliance finding its own creative spirit and energy.

But these two wings of the Republican party are now just two broken tusks. The liberal Republicans have not so much been routed as decomposed by their own inanition; and the conservative Republicans have never reached beyond the frivolity of a kind of intellectually disordered nihilism. An elephant cannot roll logs with broken tusks, and a party with two such broken tusks cannot hope to move the country in this century. For this is in the end the question to which we must come: Why does the Republican party seem hardly to belong to its own time, or even to its own place?

It is at this level that the folk memory works most deeply. Whenever the people give the Republican party its chance, it is not so much its specific policies that are found objectionable—although the accumulation of these can tell strongly in the final accounting. By its actions, it leaves a deeper feeling of malaise that the Republican party simply does not belong to the country as the people know it from day to day: how it breathes, lives, and has its being.

Does it belong in government? Or even in Washington?

THE PARTIES

A real estate agent in Washington said not long ago, "The real estate position in this city may be simply put: the Republicans always rent, and the Democrats never leave." For more than a generation now, the Republicans have come to Washington like aliens to a city where they know they will not be at home. They hardly unpack their suitcases. They live in curious places that are not really Washington, but seem to have been sewn on to it. One could hear the sigh of relief in November 1976 from the four thousand or so Republicans who would leave the follow January with the administration they had served. At last they could go home.

But a political party that feels alien in the nation's capital is a party that must be alien in the country as a whole. It is as deep as this in their souls, that the Republicans must go in the years of self-inquisition that lie ahead. It was shown in 1976 that it cannot patch the West to the Sun Belt to the South, and imagine that there is the nation. The sense of the historical nation—which itself votes in part from its folk memory—cannot be found in this way. The nation is more than a patchwork of its sections, sewn together for the occasion. Perhaps what is most remarkable about the Republican party is that for a party that is supposed to be conservative it is almost completely deficient in historical imagination. It does not seem to know its country, like it, or belong to it; its usual political behavior is a strangely un-American activity.

The Urbane and
the Primitive

IT CAN BE SAID, without fear of much contradiction, that no other great political party in any of the Western democracies has had so inglorious a record as the Republican party in the past half-century. Indeed, for most of a century that is now in its last quarter, the record has been inglorious. At the Republican National Convention in 1976, the past of the party was represented by three losers: Barry Goldwater and Nelson Rockefeller, and none other than Alf Landon. Of these three, Landon in 1936 and Goldwater in 1964 had led the party to two of its worst defeats; and as Rockefeller himself said, he had sought his party's nomination for sixteen years, and had always lost it.

The one winner, still alive, of whom the Republican party can boast, Richard Nixon, was not invited to the convention, was not celebrated, was not even mentioned. He had twice won the White House for the party; but the party was obliged to disown him.

It hardly needs the art of caricature to imagine a Republican party toast to those who have carried its banner since Theodore Roosevelt: "I give you, ladies and gentlemen, the party of Warren Harding . . . (*applause*) . . . of Calvin Coolidge . . . (*the cheers gather*) . . . of Herbert Hoover . . . (*feet drum the floor*) . . . of Alf Landon . . . (*the audience rises*) . . . of Wendell Willkie . . . (*huzzas break across the room*) . . . of Thomas Dewey . . . (*the eyes of strong men prick*) . . . of Thomas Dewey again . . . (*tears flow down flushed cheeks*) . . . of Dwight Eisenhower . . . (*cheers lift the rafters*) . . . of Dwight Eisenhower again . . . (*a roar shakes the room*) . . . of Richard Nixon . . . (*guests stand on their chairs*) . . . of Barry Goldwater . . . (*there is a stampede*) . . . of Richard Nixon again . . . (*shouts of 'four more years'*) . . . And in their line, ladies and gentlemen, I give you the leader who in 1976 showed that our party may still enjoy a present as illustrious as its past." The guests collapse.

Even the most disinterested observer—even the most concerned Republican—must conclude that there is something wrong with a great party that has a record like that. Not since Theodore Roosevelt has the Republican party had one great leader, and hardly one who has not in one way or another been inept.

Even some Republicans draw the line as far back as Theodore Roosevelt. Here is the voice of Robert Humphreys, writing on December 31, 1958, to Leonard Hall, one of the regular party leaders and then chairman of its national committee: "The Republican Party as a majority party began to die when Theodore Roosevelt died." Here is Jacob Javits, the senior Republican senator from New York, and one of the most consistent winners for his party in unfriendly territory, writing in 1964: "Following the Theodore Roosevelt era, the progressive spirit in the Republican Party steadily declined." And here is the Ripon Society, a group of earnest young Republicans, saying in 1968 that the gulf between the Republican party and the intellectual and professional community in the nation "first began to open when Theodore Roosevelt left party ranks in 1912. . . . It is a gulf which, as Walter Lippmann has written, is 'at the root of the Republican decline.'" Always the eyes are cast back, far back, to before the First World War.

Right-wing Republicans will at once protest that these are all voices of liberal Republicans, who were the custodians of the party during much of the period; and they have a point, since the record of ineptness and defeat has been compiled largely under the leadership of the "liberal" or "moderate" or "progressive" Republicans. But it still cannot be denied that the leadership of the party since Theodore Roosevelt has been consistently without luster.

Even when the Republican party has pulled off a victory in recent years, it has not won in such a way that it may be regarded as having replaced the Democrats, in the eyes of the electors, as the normal governing party of the country. Sixty-four years after the defection of Theodore Roosevelt, it is simply not a popular party, which is another way of saying that it is not yet genuinely a governing party. The point is, not that it does not or cannot ever win, or that it may not again rally, but that it wins, when it does, without any real conviction in its own cause.

Without any real conviction, even, that it has its own right to victory. Speaker after speaker at the Republican National Convention in 1976 announced that the Republican party is the minority party in the country. It is understandable that the conservatives—the right wing of the party—should feel embattled in a hostile land; but that the whole party should feel so besieged is altogether different. After all, in the quarter century since 1952, it had by 1976 won four of six presidential elections; yet it seems to have come no more into possession of the land, in that time, than when Dewey was trounced by Truman in 1948.

The backward glance to Theodore Roosevelt is a backward glance over a century in which the Republican party even now does not feel at home. This is what is astonishing and hard to explain. In many ways, the tides of both informed and public opinion are running in its favor, as the fourth quarter of the century begins. Not only the United States but the Western world in general is disposed to be more conservative than in the two previous quarters. Yet the Republican party seems unable to ride these tides with any certainty. The climate of opinion is made for it today, yet in that climate it still seems to find the strength only to droop, and draw only poison from the air.

It reminds one of what Ortega y Gasset said of the city

of Ávila, the symbol of the Spain he loved, but of which he despaired in its decay: that it is like a rosebush with its roots in the air, and its blossoms underground. The Republican party is always talking of its grassroots strength; the conservatives especially are always speaking of the grassroots support for their philosophy. But from these roots, so exposed and so visible, so picked over to prove that a majority is emerging, there comes no bloom, and so no fruit. It is as if the Republican party keeps looking the wrong way up at itself.

Before it looks for support, it needs to look at itself. No one today really knows—not even the Republicans one asks—what the Republican party has been or done in the past half century. That was the most important difference between the two vice-presidential candidates in 1976: Walter Mondale reminded people immediately of what the Democratic party has done and been; but there was nothing in Robert Dole to tell people what the Republican party has done and been. In so far as he was representative of it, Dole was the spokesman of a party that seems not to have been fertilized by the times in which it exists and must act, certainly not to have been cross-fertilized. When he said that the world wars in this century had been "Democrat wars," he was saying more than he realized: that the Republicans have sat out the twentieth century.

We must begin with a distinction; it is crucial and it will work its way in and out of our story. A *party* is not a *movement;* or perhaps how it needs to be put to some Republicans is that a movement is not a party. It is certainly true that a party that is constantly beset by assault from a movement within itself finds it difficult to act as a party, to win or to recover from defeat. The conservatives have for more than a generation been a movement within the Republican party. They have been what the French since their revolution have called internal émigrés, not leaving the country, but staying in it, disgruntled and disruptive, and with no genuine hope of victory.

Movements tend to be ideological; parties tend not to be ideological. Movements tend to have a single purpose; parties tend to have many purposes. In movements the key workers tend to be amateurs; in parties they tend to be regulars. Movements are zealous to capture their party; parties are ambitious to capture office. Movements tend to be willing for the sake of their causes to invite defeat; parties tend to be willing to subdue their causes for the sake of victory. The word we may use of movements is *primitive;* the word we may use of parties is *urbane.*

The Goldwater campaign in 1964 was a primitive movement; and so, within the Democratic party eight years later, was the McGovern campaign. The Willkie campaign in 1940 was the successful eruption of a primitive movement; and in 1976 the Reagan campaign was merely the primitive movement led by Goldwater returning to make a second effort, and to be held back at the pass only by the strenuous effort of an incumbent president who represented the urbane party.

What is most obvious is that whenever one of these movements has captured or seriously divided a party that party has lost the election. This does not mean, of course, that the urbane party leadership does not also lose elections; and one reason for the persistent strength of the conservative movement in the Republican party is the long record of defeat the party has suffered, since the New Deal, under its conventional leadership, a record that is not made to look any better by mentioning the victories of Eisenhower and Nixon, neither of whom left the party in better shape than he found it. At least a priori, the conservatives have a case. But it is even more clear that when they capture a party, movements do not win elections. In capturing the party, they have already defined themselves so rigidly that they have excluded the voters whose support they then most need to attract.

Moreover, when a movement takes itself outside one or other of the main parties, it does no better, whether the Bull Moose movement in 1912, or the Henry Wallace movement in 1944, or the George Wallace movement when he put himself forward as an Independent. Any attempt by the conservatives in the Republican party to form a third party would fare no better, which is at least one reason why, in spite of their restlessness, they have remained as internal émigrés in a party whose urbanity they despise, as in fact they despised the urbane leadership of Ford in 1976.

21

THE PARTIES

It is often said that the parties in America today are weak, and are getting weaker. But there is no real evidence for this. Their character as institutions has changed; they can no longer attract and hold support in the same ways as before; fewer voters identify themselves automatically with one or other of the main parties; ticket-splitting seems to be more of a habit. In spite of all this, and much else, the parties go on. Their resilience is striking. Indeed, given the weakness of the national structures of American parties between presidential elections, given that they meet as national parties in convention only once every four years (unless the Democratic experiment of a midterm convention in 1974 and again in 1978 becomes a custom), what is amazing is that they cohere at all, and survive so well. It is noticeable that the conservatives now are thinking of capturing the Republican party and not of forming a party of their own.

Whenever it has suffered a serious reverse in the past half century, the Republican party has meddled with the idea of disbanding and re-forming itself as another party with another label. Before the midterm elections of 1938, Arthur Vandenberg was actively promoting the idea of forming a new coalition party with those Democrats who were disaffected with Franklin Roosevelt's administration and its measures. Yet in the elections, the Republican party itself did well. After it had won a second presidential election in succession in 1956, L. Brent Bozell wrote in the *National Review* that "The answer [for conservatives], if there is any, probably lies in a third party. But that development must await the death of one of the major parties." Since the Democrats have never shown any intention of giving up the ghost, Bozell was looking forward to the decease of the Republican Party, as many conservatives still do.

The simple fact is that the Republicans do not cherish their own party as do the Democrats, and there is evidence for this. For thirty-six years, the national structure of the Republican party, in spite of intermittent attempts to strengthen it, has been lamentably weak: much weaker than that of the Democratic party, even when the Democrats have suffered severe defeats. In saying "for thirty-six years," one is of course placing the initial responsibility on the Willkie campaign of 1940, on a primitive movement that was to a significant extent allowed its head by the urbane leadership of the party; and it will be shown that in that campaign, both for the nomination and in the election, were sown the seeds of many of the troubles of the Republican party since then.

It is not from the New Deal that the Republican party has not recovered, but from the nomination in 1940 of one of the most preposterous figures ever to lead a major party; and it is more than interesting that he led it as a self-professed liberal or moderate Republican.

We are about to turn to him, but for the moment the general point may be made. What was absent from Gerald Ford's campaign for the nomination, and then in the election, was a strong party organization on which he could draw as the incumbent president. With his nomination at last won, there was still no strong party structure to which he could reach. No one knew where, or in whom, it existed to any purpose or with any efficiency. An incumbent president had to begin to create his party a mere seventy-three days before the election, even after that party had been in power for eight years, and he himself for two. Elephants are known not to be very bright, but it is rather demeaning of the species to suggest that they are naturally as dumb as that.

One returns to *The Emerging Republican Majority,* with its forecast of "a dominant Republican Party based in the Heartland, South and California," set against "a minority Democratic Party based in the Northeast and the Pacific Northwest." It is the crudity of such a prediction, such a weighing of votes, that is breathtaking. The Republicans, Phillips said, "can easily afford to lose the states of Massachusetts, New York, and Michigan." But the fact is that in 1976, when the thesis was put to its first serious test, the Republican party could not "easily afford" to lose Massachusetts and New York. No party can afford to throw away great chunks of the country in advance like that.

But neither can anyone begin to form a winning strategy for a party merely by adding up regions and blocs of voters, until he is sure that there is a party there for which to devise a strategy; and why the thesis of *The Emerging Republican Majority* is so interesting, in the hour of its failure, is that it is representative of so many others in that its author hardly talks about the Republican party at all, whether to ask what it is, or what it ought to be. There are merely blocks of voters, and techniques which are supposed to attract them. But this is not enough.

The Boy Prodigy As Prodigious Fool

IF ONE WISHES TO retain one's judgment, one will try to resist the impression that the two major parties in the United States exist at, and for, the pleasure of Walter Cronkite: that they are created by him every four years, out of the aery region over which he presides, playthings for his sport, puppets into which he breathes life. Anyone who saw him, in 1976, pat Nelson Rockefeller on the knee, must have wondered why he did not just take the vice-president on to his lap. Parties have histories longer than the flickering memories of television reporters. They have their own tenacious lives, and their pasts do not just evaporate.

The Republican party today is still the party that was shattered not in 1932 but in 1936. After its devastating defeat in that year, John Hamilton as the chairman of its national committee took the party in hand. By the time the nomination campaigns began in 1939, he had rebuilt the party, much as Robert Strauss rebuilt the Democratic party between 1972 and 1976. The debts from the previous election had been repaid. Republicans had done well in the midterm elections in 1938. On the other side, the Democrats were in trouble and vulnerable. The enthusiasm for the New Deal had been dissipated; the deserters from it included men as symbolically if not, by then, actually as important as James Farley and John Garner; war had broken out in Europe and was threatening the United States; there was the issue of a third term for Roosevelt. This was an election the Republicans "ought" to have won; it was well placed to win. But the chance of victory was thrown away by the Willkie movement; Hamilton's work was destroyed in a few months.

It was then that the habit—the psychology—of defeat became ingrained in the Republican party. But the persistence of this habit—and this psychology—was ensured by one aspect of the Willkie campaign in 1940: the reckless destruction, by him and his supporters, of the national committee of the party.

The fact that Willkie was a liberal Republican—indeed, had been registered as a Democrat only a few years before —and that he had the support of what is now called the Establishment of the party, does not alter the fact that he won the nomination primarily as a result of the grassroots activity of the amateurs in the Willkie Clubs. Thus nominated by the primitives, Willkie at once began to behave like one, and with his own brash naïveté and amateurishness he ran one of the most incompetent election campaigns in history.

His first act as his party's nominee was to remove Hamilton from the chairmanship of the national committee. In fact, Willkie's first idea, if it can be called such, was to do without a national chairman at all. With no political experience, never having fought an election before, having no intimate acquaintance with any of the party's leaders, he desperately needed the national committee and its tried and proved chairman. Instead he replaced him with Joseph Martin, the Minority Leader in the House of Representatives, who was burdened with his duties there, did not know how to run a national campaign, and developed no strategy, either for the party or for the candidate to whom it had given birth in a fit of absence of mind.

But this was not all. Even before he removed Hamilton, Willkie had formed an advisory committee for his campaign under the chairmanship of Harold Stassen, who thus began his long and intimate association with failure. Willkie allowed the national committee to have three

26

members on this committee, but it was already nervous of him, and the removal of Hamilton had only alienated it more. From start to finish, there was no effective supervision of the campaign.

Willkie moved from disastrous to yet more disastrous decisions. He continued to ignore the national committee. Off his own bat, he announced that the party would in the whole campaign spend even less than the maximum permitted by the Hatch Act, even though it was out of office and needed the most widespread campaign it could mount. He allowed the Willkie Clubs, which had given him the nomination, to continue as an independent organization in the election campaign; and even more absurdly, he allowed another new organization, Democrats for Willkie, to enjoy the same autonomy. Even though he was Willkie's nominee as chairman, Martin had no control over these amateurs; and regular party organizations, such as the Young Republicans, were embittered and frustrated by their amateur and undirected rivals.

As one Republican leader was to put it: "It was bad enough for our local party workers to see a bunch of amateurs try to direct the campaign, but it was too much to have these same people ask for voter lists and precinct data which local workers had spent so much time to secure." This rift was never closed—Willkie seems hardly to have been aware of it—and again one is reminded of other primitive campaigns: Goldwater's in 1964, and McGovern's in 1972.

George Sokolosky, one of the more intelligent campaigners for Willkie, was later to say: "The organization was left to novices and amateurs. Every suggestion as to policy and tactics made to the candidate by the more experienced party leaders was, in the final implementation, ignored. The amateurs surrounded Mr. Willkie in a tight cordon through which it became increasingly more difficult to send either ideas, criticism, or suggestions. . . . A campaign is not a crusade and not won by noise in unison but by enthusiastic and coordinated competence. The latter was lacking throughout." This is always what happens when the primitives are allowed to take command.

But what matters to us, more than a generation later, is that the national committee of the Republican Party, the body ultimately representing its national organization, has never recovered its prestige within the party since the injury inflicted on it by Willkie. It has had some good and competent chairmen since then, but in the end it has always seemed to be a party without the steady resource of an effective organization. It is true that the national organizations of the major parties have always been weaker in the United States than elsewhere, but this does not mean that they do not matter. Whenever they have been weaker than usual, that party has normally lost.

Of all the reasons why Gerald Ford, as the incumbent president, had such difficulty in securing the nomination of his own party in 1976, and in conducting an effective election campaign in time, none was more important than the lack of prestige, within its own party, from which the Republican National Committee has suffered since 1940. After all, the power of the Committee to Re-elect the President in 1972 was exercised by a man as distant from the regular party organization as John Mitchell, in the absence of a national committee of prestige or influence. If it is conservative Republicans, such as Goldwater and Reagan, who have recently set their primitives against the urbane party organization, they can at least claim that the path was blazed by an avowed liberal, new to the party, Wendell Willkie.

Parties, if used, are strong. Parties, if invited, are hardworking. Parties, if trusted, are loyal. Parties, if encouraged, are resilient. Parties are shepherds; they round up the flock, count its heads, and do not let either the sheep or the goats stray too far between elections. Moreover, in doing all this, they also help to stimulate and retain some sense of common purpose and life in the party, which has something to do with the causes and interests for which it fights, but something also to do with its sense of itself as an organization, with a persistence and vitality of its own.

Rub the Republican party, and one's fingers can feel no fiber. Gaze on a Republican convention, no matter the year, and its delegates and alternates seem to have been to a theatrical costumier. The party is like a circus elephant, with a bonnet on its head and a frilly skirt round the folds of its dropping abdomen. Silly hats and ribbons and jingling baubles are a part of the conventions of both parties;

they are not to be despised. But at a Republican convention they do not seem to be an assertion of the characters of the delegates, proceeding from a conviction in themselves as Republicans. They seem instead to be a part of the delegates' role-playing as Republicans. They deck themselves out as Republicans, as if to prove that they know what it means to be Republican, as if to persuade even themselves why they are Republicans.

It is not enough even that they are veterans: bars of metal must spill down their lapels to prove that they are veterans. If it is true that there have been "Democrat wars" in this century, how strange that it is the Republicans who advertise their participation in them. Even as veterans, they seem to play a role. The delegates at Republican conventions are dressed like Christmas trees; one wishes one knew what they are celebrating.

There are two kinds of people: those who define themselves by their roles, and find their security in these; and those who define themselves by the awareness of their own natures, and find their security there. It is not unimportant that, in general, the Republicans seem to be the former, and that their party, therefore, seems to lack fiber also. A man whose personality was vibrant, complex, and rich, such as Everett Dirksen, stood out almost as an exception among them, whereas in the party of their opponents he would have been one among many, perhaps not even to be particularly noticed as a character.

A long-standing and loyal Republican on the Hill, when asked about this, said with a shake of his head: "The criticism is deadly, but I have to agree with it, at least a lot of the way. The Republican party today does not have a very strong personality, and that is one of the things wrong with it. If it and the Democratic party came into a room at a party, I'll admit that it would be the Democratic party I would want to talk to all evening, even though I then went home with the Republican party I'm married to." And one does indeed feel that, whereas the Democrats love their party as a beautiful and worthy mistress, the Republicans are stuck with their own party in a laudable but dull marriage of unrewarding convenience.

What is more, it is the conservative Republicans who will agree with this more than the liberal Republicans.

There is at least something knotty in the right-wing Republicans, from Robert Taft to Goldwater to Reagan. But all those unknotty liberal Republicans, to each of whom we will come, what are we to make of their spinelessness? Perhaps they have been in the past and today still are such feeble standard-bearers of their party because they do not believe, passionately or determinedly, that it is necessary for their party to be in power. And perhaps they lack this conviction because, on the whole, they are not dissatisfied with a Democratic regime.

It is in this context that more must be said of Willkie. Here we can see, near to the beginning of our story, the connection between political character (or the lack of it) and political belief (or the lack of it). In his diaries, Henry Wallace tells that at a luncheon at the White House on May 22, 1943, Winston Churchill said "Willkie reminded him of a Newfoundland dog, rushing into the water, and coming out again, shaking himself, jumping up on the ladies and putting his paws on their shoulders, wagging his tail and sweeping all the dishes off the table at the same time." At which Franklin Roosevelt quoted Mme. Chiang Kai-shek, whose judgments of political character were at least feline, as saying that Willkie was a "perpetual adolescent"; and returning to this story a generation later, these are still one's impressions, in fact the kindliest of them.

Willkie was a poseur; in every essential, he was a role-player. Olsen and Johnson, then at the height of their popularity as entertainers, met him once, and announced that they would vote for him because he was a "born actor." Roosevelt seems to have played with him, affecting a measure of admiration and even of affection, but more amused by him than anything else. The memoirs and diaries about Roosevelt, kept mostly by men who were themselves of strong and individual characters, have to be read with care: He said what he thought would please his hearers, while reserving his true judgment to himself. "We may still have Willkie with us," he said at the beginning of 1944, leaving Wallace to decipher what he meant.

Between 1940 and 1944, Roosevelt kept Willkie on a string, patting him now and then, exactly as if he were a dog. After Willkie had died, Roosevelt told Wallace that "he did not think Willkie was really a liberal." The hard-core New Dealers, such as Harold Ickes, were contemptuous of the man. Eleanor Roosevelt told Wallace that she did not think much of him, and Ickes leaped at every chance to go after the man *Fortune,* even while promoting his candidacy, had described as "the Mississippi Yankee, the clever bumpkin, the homespun, cracker-barrel simplifier of national issues," which is not quite the way one speaks of a savior come out of the West to lead the nation to its redemption.

If one wants to find Willkie at his boldest, setting the mold for the liberal Republicans who were to follow, it is in his remark about Stalin, after he had met the Russian leader: "About the man himself, there is no need to be cautious. He is one of the most significant men of his generation." Now, that is insight! That is courage! No wonder that Churchill said that "Stalin saw through Willkie at once." It does not take much, when a man is so transparent.

As he addressed himself to the already growing problem of Arab nationalism and the Palestine issue, Willkie said: "The pragmatic, realistic truth lies in the middle." That is the liberal Republican: caught not with his trousers down, but with them up, as clothed as he ever is. In Willkie, the liberal Republican was finding his voice: the adamant statement of positions he has not defined, on difficult issues about which his convictions are irresolute. Willkie "is spiritually most photogenic," said William Allen White, who was a master of damning his fellow Republicans with words of praise for which he could not be reproached; and he had about said it all.

This is not just history. With Willkie we are on the threshold of our own time. Although he came out of the Midwest and was carried to the nomination by the primitives in the party's rank and file, he was sponsored from about 1937 onward by the eastern Establishment press, from the *New York Times* to the Luce publications. In spite of his soothing liberal language about business, his own business record could not bear strict examination— White said that in this respect he needed to claim a statute of limitations—and his connections with Wall Street were close. Harry Truman in his memoirs reminds us that during the hearings on the Public Utility Holding Bill in 1935 —whose purpose was "to destroy the cartels through which the power trusts were able to maintain exorbitant rates" and establish some public supervision of them— among the financiers who came down to Washington to testify against the bill were "the Whitneys of the New York Stock Exchange," John Foster Dulles, and of course Willkie, whose own utilities holding company, the Commonwealth and Pacific, was often ruthless in its exercise of political power through its subsidiary companies.

Wilkie was "not really a liberal," as Roosevelt said, yet the strategy of him and his supporters was to get returned to power by masquerading as one. His lack of political character and his lack of political principle were joined, and this has all too obviously been the weakness of the liberal Republicans ever since, the reason why they have remained generally as pulpy and as disingenuous as their first standard-bearer after the New Deal. When Javits, an honorable man in a difficult position, says that "the change for the better" in the Republican party, to a more progressive spirit, "dates from 1940, with the nomination of Wendell Willkie," he is in fact underlining the bankruptcy of the liberal wing of the party since then. By 1976 this wing was virtually absent from the Republican convention in Kansas City.

What *was* Willkie, and what *is* he now in the folk memory of the Republican party? Who now thinks about him? Yet he led his party, and aspired to lead it again, at crucial moments in 1940 and 1944, as the Second World War broke across the world, and at a time of real opportunity for the Republicans, when the impetus of the New Deal was almost exhausted. He must mean something to the party today, but search as one may, his influence is impossible to find, except that it is from the characterless and unprincipled example of this man that the liberal Republicans have since taken their model.

In his poem "Washington in July," Robert Lowell says that "the elect and the elected" come there "bright as dimes," and stay until they are "soft and dishevelled." The trouble with Willkie was that although in some respects he was "bright as a dime" when he chose to rush on Washington, bounding to the sport, he was also more than a little dishevelled; and if one gazes from him, across the years, to the crumpled figures of the liberal Republicans today, their dishevelment seems, as with him, to be a part of their nature: dishevelled in mind and spirit, and above all in belief.

Twice Backing the
Same Loser

MOST OBSERVERS OF THE Republican National Convention in 1976 remarked on the pitiable array of the liberal
leadership of the party. Old and young, they were like
whipped dogs. The grin of Nelson Rockefeller had grown
slack; and slack was the face of Harold Stassen, the "boy
governor" of Minnesota in the 1940s; slack the pudgy,
overfattened smile of Charles Percy, the junior senator
from Illinois, who was once hailed as the future hope of
his party; slack the bearing, if one allows it such a description, of Elliott Richardson, who has drifted from office to
office, leaving the mark, less of any achievement, than of a
reputation which even he seems to begin to realize is mis-
placed; slack now the charm of Edward Brooke, the senior
senator from Massachusetts; slack the posturing of Hugh
Scott, at last retiring as the Minority Leader of the Senate:
slack and hangdog, all of them, weak and tiresome men.

Some were only weary, like Javits, still urging his un-
heeding party to have some compassion; or scornful of the
pass to which their party had come, like Clifford Case. His
erectness was isolated, reminding one of the flinty honor of
a man such as George Aiken of Vermont, not so long ago a
senator, in whom the liberal leadership of the party found

a posture that was telling. But the party did not listen to Javits; it did not want to hear from Case. The liberal Republicans were there only to accept without public protest the nomination of one conservative as the presidential candidate of the party, and another as the vice-presidential candidate. In order to hold off Reagan, they would let mediocrity run with mediocrity.

How did it come to this? After the full impact of the Depression and then of the New Deal had been felt, the Republican party in 1936 looked not to the East and the cities for a candidate, but to the Midwest and small-town and still rural America. As the candidate of his party in that year, Alf Landon was by no means a political fool, although that is what his popular reputation is likely to remain as the result of his crushing defeat. But equally he was not much of a strategist, a campaigner, or a leader. While the country waited to hear from him after his nomination, Westbrook Pegler posted him as a missing person, and issued the following description: "Height: average. Weight: average. Complexion: average. Habits: average. Birthmarks and scars: average." When at last he did begin to campaign, he was still average, pathetically enlisted to challenge the campaigning genius of Roosevelt.

His candidacy was initially promoted by a group of men from the Kansas City *Star,* the Arkansas City *Traveler,* the El Dorado *Times,* the Salina *Journal,* the Topeka *Journal,* and the Iola *Register,* which do not together constitute what is generally meant by the eastern Establishment press. In fact, in spite of the dedicated labors of John Hamilton as chairman of the Republican National Committee, the Eastern leadership of the party was demoralized in 1936, not only by the Depression and the unnerving impact of the first four years of the New Deal but by the inroads the Democrats had begun to make, first in 1928 and then in 1932, into what until then had been regarded as the Republican strongholds in their own territory.

In spite of the fact that Hamilton and Frank Knox, who was Landon's running mate, believed they were engaged in "rebuilding a conservative party," the Republican campaign in 1936 was the first to lay down the strategy of the conventional leadership of the party for the next twenty-eight years. The basis of that strategy was to hold the Republican vote, which had remained solid even in 1932; to attract the agricultural vote, which was disaffected by the Agricultural Adjustment Act; and above all to win back the progressive Republicans, the Independents, and the disgruntled Democrats who had helped give Roosevelt his first majority. In accordance with this strategy, the Republican platform was "definitely liberal," said William Allen White: "Much less liberal than Landon had asked, but much less conservative than his Eastern friends had hoped for."

The comment of this shrewd if sometimes opportunist Republican editor is interesting, because the eastern leadership of the party in 1936 was still perceived as conservative. As early as August 10, 1935, Landon himself had said that although people were turning against Roosevelt, "they are also just as much opposed to the old-guard leadership of the Republican Party," meaning exactly its conservative and Eastern leadership. It was in the Midwest that Republicanism had been daubed by the progressive brush.

But it was after the overwhelming defeat that was inflicted on the first tentative "me-too" strategy of Landon that the change could be seen to begin, as the Eastern leadership moved, not to reject but to embrace and reinforce "me-tooism." After the election, the *Washington Post,* then an Eastern newspaper in the Republican camp, proclaimed: "The liberal direction which Mr. Landon has given to Republicanism augurs well for a further regeneration." But even more illuminating was the alarm of some of the party leaders in the East at the erosion of the very foundations of their power in the big industrial states. It was now that an ideological and geographical rift began to develop.

A month after the election, Hamilton Fish, as Eastern Establishment a voice as one could wish, told the Republican State Committee of New York: "For sixteen years the party that we belong to has invariably fought Franklin D. Roosevelt and Governor Lehman, and the result has been that we have not elected a Governor in sixteen years. . . . I want to keep the door open and not shut it to the wage earners and the liberals." At the same meeting, another voice of the Eastern Establishment, Laurens Hamilton, envisaged for the Republicans only "the important work that is done under our form of government by an opposition party."

The voices of the East were soon like a chorus. Harold G. Hoffman, the governor of New Jersey, said that "the Republican Party is hampered by leaders who are still living among cobwebs and mothballs." Even John Hamilton, who was still working to rebuild a conservative party, confided, "I think that the Republicans will have to recognize . . . that they have lost the pulse of the people." Nicholas Murray Butler, undoubtedly a dean of the Eastern Establishment, declared: "There isn't any Republican Party anymore, and there hasn't been a Republican Party for a long time." Out of their frustration, the editors of *Fortune,* a politically more significant journal than now, asked, "What can the Republicans do?", and answered, "They can disappear."

Out of this despair was born, primarily in the East, the philosophy (if it can be dignified as such) and the strategy of the liberal Republicans, which were to carry the party from defeat to defeat, until it plucked a general back from his military assignment in Europe to try to save it from extinction. "When the Democratic Party was at its most unhappy, it at least had a home," moaned the editors of *Fortune* in February 1937, meaning the South and the great city machines. The real condemnation of the liberal leadership of the Republican party in the succeeding forty years is that it still does not have "a home" in this sense. In the battle between Ford and Reagan at Kansas City in 1976, it was still two homes, divided against each other.

On April 27, 1937, in a letter to John Hamilton, Landon crushed an attempt by Herbert Hoover to call a special party convention to consider Republican policy, saying that it would be a meeting of "ghosts from the boneyard." In another letter, on September 13, he said: "If you had a Republican convention, who would you have as the front row on the platform?"; and after reciting the names of Hoover and his associates, he snapped: "Read 'em and weep." Hamilton turned with skill, and with a conservative but not reactionary intent, to rebuild the shattered party, only to have his work destroyed in one summer, as we have seen, by the eruption of Wendell Willkie.

Willkie had stepped into the vacuum that was all that

the once powerful Eastern and liberal leadership of the party had created in the eight years since its first defeat by Roosevelt. From 1940 to 1944, it was just as paralyzed, and in 1944 and again in 1948 it could bring forward no more inspiring figure than Thomas Dewey. One of the tests of a governing class in the past has been its ability to throw up leaders who were at least fit to govern on its behalf; that must also be one of the tests of a party leadership. The Republican party in the past forty years has seemed to have no nurseries, and with the diminishing of its numbers out in the states, this condition is likely to become worse. What is interesting about the continued support the party leadership gave to Dewey for so many years is that one cannot even now see other men it might have chosen. The nurseries were even then not bringing forward the rivals who might have contended with Dewey, just as they were not twenty years later to bring forward rivals able to contend with Nixon.

What is one to say of Dewey, who can hardly be blamed for losing the election in 1944, in the middle of a war, but can certainly be blamed for losing it in 1948? What can one say of him except that, once again the nomination of the Eastern Establishment of the party underlined the connection between (lack of) political character and (lack of) political belief. In 1940, Wolcott Gibbs caught him in the *New Yorker:* "His face has a compressed appearance, as though someone had squeezed it in a vise. His suits are custom-made but uninteresting, and always seem a little too tight for him. . . . He is a hard man to imagine in a toga." A Republican woman four years later sharpened the criticism: "You have to know Dewey to dislike him." Eight years later, another Republican woman, Lillian Dykastra, wrote home from the Republican Convention at which Dewey had organized the nomination of Eisenhower: "[Dewey] is just about the nastiest little man I've ever known. He struts sitting down." In one of his campaigns, a man in the crowd had shouted to him, "Smile, Governor," and Dewey had replied, "I thought I was"; and that about says it all.

Dewey entered the convention in 1944 to the playing of "Mine eyes have seen the glory of the coming of the Lord," which, as I. F. Stone observed at the time, "was laying it on a bit thick." He was a little man at what Adlai Stevenson had already called "a time for greatness," but a presumptuous one—in a letter to a friend on September 16, 1943, Taft described a meeting at which "Tom Dewey arrived in a private car with a bodyguard and was so arrogant that he made all the Republicans mad"—and what one really wants to know is why the Eastern Establishment of the Republican party, from 1940, when he first entered a campaign for the nomination, until 1952, when he engineered the nomination of Eisenhower, allowed him such prominence in the party: this man of whom Taft justifiably said that he had "no real courage," who in all his long career seemed to be guided by no perceptible political principle, and was rightly described at the time as "a cautious and fairly accurate opinion sampler," but even in that not accurate enough when it mattered.

Is it any wonder that the conservative Republicans, who watched this man unnecessarily confuse the issue against Willkie in 1940, then lead the party to defeat twice in succession, then in 1952 muster the Eastern Establishment to reach outside the party for a candidate who cared very little for it—is it any wonder that they not only hold him in perhaps more contempt than any other urbane Republican, with the possible exception of Rockefeller, but contemn also the leadership that placed and sustained him in a position of such power and influence? Can one imagine the leadership of the Democratic party clinging so demeaningly to so consistently proven a loser?

"Both platforms on which I ran in 1944 and 1948," Dewey said later, "were generally good and progressive documents. On the other hand, some provisions of both platforms were so vague on some points, as a result of compromise, as to justify the frequent assertion that the platform means what the candidate says it means." It is an honest enough statement, but what did he say the platforms meant, either in 1944 or in 1948? What did Dewey ever stand for during one of the most important decades in the twentieth century? If the Republican party were to inscribe a tablet of its beliefs today, what one sentence, what one aspiration, what one strategy, would be taken from the collected papers of Thomas Dewey?

As one political journalist had said of him in 1940, he seemed to have "completely missed . . . the very emotion of the past thirty years." Leveled at him, this is also the criticism that must be leveled at the liberal leadership of the party as it fastened its grip on the levers of power in the 1940s. As well as self-knowledge, said Disraeli, a statesman must also have a knowledge of "the spirit of the age" even if he opposes it, as a conservative may well choose to do. He must know it and understand it. This knowledge of the spirit of the age ran deep in a conservative such as Winston Churchill: In spite of all his antiquated notions, he always seemed to belong to his own time, to be a modern man. The torment of the twentieth century was his own torment. When the British ambassador to Greece complained in 1944 that he felt as if he were living on the side of a volcano, Churchill sent back a cable asking him where he expected to be living in an age such as our own. One cannot imagine such a response being sent by Dewey, or by any of the liberal Republicans of the past half century.

One can find this readiness to live in his own age in the words and actions of Harry Truman; one can find it even, in the 1940s before he really arrived on the national scene, in the early papers of Adlai Stevenson. One can also find it in other Republicans: in William Borah, for example, and certainly in Robert Taft, who confronted the great issues of the age with a tenacious if not always clearminded attempt at honesty. To put it in a nutshell: In 1940 both Arthur Vandenberg and Thomas Dewey were candidates for the nomination of their party, both were then isolationists, and under the impact of the Second World War both became internationalists. But although there was more than a little of the pompous ass in Vandenberg—Taft's wife once wrote to her sons, ". . . your father urged me to butter Van up. I tried manfully, but he buttered himself so thoroughly that I couldn't find an ungreased spot"—one feels that his conversion was at least real to him, that the issue was personal, and that his decision was therefore difficult and deliberate, so that it then counted in the life of the nation; whereas the conversion of Dewey seems to have been no more than a slither from one convenient position to another.

It is too easy to say that politicians lose because of circumstances they cannot influence, or mistakes they might have avoided. More often than not, they are unable to influence the circumstances, or incapable of avoiding the mistakes, because they lack conviction. The political character is uninformed by political principle, and so the political ambition is undirected by any true political motive. In each of Dewey's three attempts to lead his party in the 1940s, one can detect this flaw: the very flaw which in the years that have followed has reduced the Eastern leadership of the party to nerveless debilitation.

In 1940, Dewey could still be counted as right wing, and he was one of three right-wing leaders, the others being Taft and Vandenberg, seeking the Republican nomination. He has himself left his own thoughts on what then happened at the national convention: ". . . every candidate wants to show enough strength to be one of the leaders on the first ballot. He also wants to have enough strength in reserve so that he can gain on the psychologically important second ballot. For example, in 1940, I led on the first three ballots, out of six—the wrong three. I lost ground on the second ballot. That was the beginning of the end and everyone knew it." But if he knew it, he did not act accordingly.

From the point of view of the right wing of the party, of which he was then a spokesman, there can be little doubt that the nomination of Willkie might have been stopped if Dewey had withdrawn as soon as his support began to slip. After the second, and even after the third, ballot the forces of the three regular and right-wing party leaders could have made a deal: Vandenberg himself said later that "Between us we could have controlled the convention if it had been done in the first instance"; Taft had no doubt that he could have rallied the anti-Willkie forces if Dewey had backed down earlier. But it was not until the fifth ballot that Dewey signaled his surrender, and when John Bricker, the senator from Ohio, asked the chairman of the convention for a recess so that the forces of Dewey and Taft might get together, the request was refused, the sixth ballot was immediately called, and Willkie went over the top.

All of this does not just help to explain, it is essential if we are to explain the similar paralysis of the conventional or urbane leadership of the Republican party at convention after convention since then. It is not even irrelevant that Dewey's support had began to seep away in his own territory, not only before the convention but before the emergence of Willkie, and before Hitler had overrun Europe and by doing so had put the isolationists in a predicament. As a result of dissidence within the Republican party in the two states that ought to have been his most secure base, Dewey arrived at the convention having lost control of one third of the delegates from New York, and with little control over a New Jersey delegation, which was split from top to bottom by a feud between the rival candidates for the governorship. It was the dissident leaders of these delegations that led the exodus from Dewey to Willkie on the early ballots. Even in his own backyard, he could not hold the support he needed, yet he would be a spoiler, fight beyond the second ballot when "everyone knew" that he was lost, and throw the nomination to the man who ought to have been his main rival.

In 1944, Dewey had swung from isolationism to internationalism, but without any evidence of real conviction that touched the nation, and he had swung from being a critic of the New Deal to accepting it, but again without being able to communicate any sense that his conversion had been struck from a genuine change of belief. But by these conversions, he had made himself acceptable to the Eastern and liberal leadership of the party—in a word, he had become urbane—and he had so tightened his control of the Republican party in New York that he was henceforth able to use its strength mercilessly and with effect. For him to win the nomination was therefore not difficult. But how could he win the election? As a headline in the *Wall Street Journal* put it: "Statistics Favor a G.O.P. Victory: But Democrats Still Have Roosevelt."

The election campaign of 1944 is one of the few of which one might say, if one were just making a good story out of it, that it was "won" by a single speech, even by a single sentence in a single speech. Roosevelt was old and sick, and preoccupied with the war. For weeks and months he barely stirred in public to notice the election, least of all to notice his opponent. But at last the old campaigner struck; his dog had been attacked, and he went on the air to say: "I am accustomed to hearing malicious falsehoods about myself, but I think I have a right to object to libelous statements about my dog." At one stroke, as someone put it, the campaign became one of "Dewey *vs.* Fala." Dewey

42

was stung, exactly as Roosevelt had meant (and waited) to sting him, and he responded with savage attacks on the president, as the president had meant him to respond. According to Eleanor Roosevelt, her husband in the weeks that followed used to go round the White House chuckling that the Americans preferred a big man with a little dog to a little man with a big dog. Dewey owned a great dane.

Why does something like the Fala speech matter? Why is it more than a gimmick, more even than a stroke of political genius by a great campaigner? It is because Roosevelt had only to show up the emptiness of his opponent. Himself an internationalist, he did not have to answer a latecomer to internationalism; himself the creator of the New Deal, he did not have to answer a convert to the New Deal, especially when he had himself already said that it had run its course. He had only to tap the man once sharply on the head, and the hollowness that was within sent its echoes across the country. When the game of politics is played to the hilt, as Roosevelt enjoyed playing it, the seriousness of the political endeavor is often revealed in the brilliance of a single performance.

But what again is astounding is that, when the emptiness of Dewey had been exposed by a single speech about a dog, the Eastern and liberal leadership of the Republican party did not get rid of Dewey. They had picked a loser, and they stuck to the runt. It would have been a great deal better if, like a sow, they had just rolled over on the wretched creature. But instead they suckled him. Was ever a drying teat offered to such an undeserving mouth?

Whatever the other reasons why Harry Truman won in 1948, the most important is that he was, and that he was perceived by the people to be, a man of political conviction; Dewey was not. Taft's judgment may seem to be questionable because he was Dewey's rival, but no one can read the story of the 1948 election without sympathizing with his own observation: "I could have won the election if nominated. I am absolutely certain that Dewey could have won if he had put up any kind of a fight at all and dealt with the issues before the people." Harold Ickes commented that Taft was the "Babe" Ruth of the Republican party, but that with the candidacy of Dewey it had "sent in a batboy with the bases full and only one run needed." After the election, the Louisville *Courier Journal* said acidly: "No presidential candidate in the future will be so inept that four of his major speeches can be boiled down to these historic four sentences: Agriculture is important. Our rivers are full of fish. You cannot have freedom without liberty. The future lies ahead. (We might add a fifth . . . the TVA is a fine thing, and we must make certain that nothing like it ever happens again)."

Through the elections of 1940 and 1944 and 1948, the policy of "me-tooism," and the political characters of those who were its standard-bearers, had failed the Republican party. Its liberal and urbane leadership had every reason to distrust itself, the candidates it had sponsored and the policies it had put forward, and even the party as a whole, which it had fashioned with such an absence of political belief. But it must win. Regardless of the party, at whatever cost to its furure, and to its own sense of itself, the liberal leadership had to win in 1952, twenty years after the first victory of Franklin Roosevelt; and to this end it reached to a man who had never even voted in an election in his life.

Eisenhower is not easily to be despised. He proved to have a political grit and a political instinct of his own. But that does not alter the fact that, in choosing him, the Eastern Establishment of the Republican party made the decision that it should govern, but that the Republican party should not. Out of office in the 1930s and the 1940s by the decision of the electors, the Republicans were again to be out of office in the 1950s by the decision of their own Eastern leadership. On behalf of their party, the liberal Republicans abdicated in 1952; and since then every flicker of life from them has been only the twitch of a corpse. Their burial in 1976 had been self-invited, many years before.

The Surrender to
Eisenhower

IF ONE READS HIS own memoirs, and those of his associates, with the care they deserve, it is often difficult to know how seriously to take Dwight Eisenhower as a politician. He says so many things that are apparently so simple in apparently so ingenuous a manner that one has to go back and reread his words to find their import. "See Ike Run" might be the summary of all that he utters, but when one pauses actually to see Ike run, one begins to convict him, not of ingenuousness but of slyness. Innocence is not normally an attribute of a winner, and Eisenhower ran rings round his rivals with such frequency that one must in the end allow him the praise that he deserves: that he was a very knowing and cunning man in a world in which he seemed to be artless.

On the night of his own inauguration, John Kennedy talked to some friends about Eisenhower as he had observed him during the day. "The vitality of the man!" he exclaimed. "It stood out so strongly, there at the inauguration. There was Chris Herter, looking old and ashen. There was Allen Dulles, gray and tired. There was Bob Anderson, with his collar seeming two sizes too large on a shrunken neck. And there was the oldest of them all, Ike

45

—as healthy and ruddy and as vital as ever." This is not the picture of a man who had not enjoyed his eight years in the White House, who had not played the game to the limit, delighting in its "rushes and rallies, its triumphs and discomfitures." Eisenhower wanted to be president, he liked being president, and so he was president. But he was not a Republican.

He has left his own account of the visit that Henry Cabot Lodge paid him at his NATO headquarters on September 4, 1951. Lodge pointed out that the liberal or moderate leadership of the Republican party was in a state of decomposure, that the twenty-year absence of the party from power had stimulated its right wing, and accentuated the stridency of its rhetoric, that passions in the party were running high, and it was being drawn to irresponsibility, that even the two-party system was itself in danger. "You are the only one," he said to Eisenhower, "who can be elected by the Republicans to the presidency. You *must* permit the use of your name in the upcoming primaries." With a delicacy of understatement that one can savor, Eisenhower describes this visit as "significant," and adds: "I began to look anew—perhaps subconsciously—at myself and politics." Perhaps subconsciously: If one believes that, one will believe anything.

In the twenty years since Eisenhower's second victory, liberal Republicans have not got out of their heads the idea that his electoral successes could be repeated by a candidate drawn from among themselves. They have not accepted the fact that his victories were not Republican victories. "Eisenhower put Eisenhower's party in power," wrote Richard Rovere at the time; "it is the president who has the mandate, not the Republican party." Emmet John Hughes, one of Eisenhower's shrewdest advisors, has written that "this electoral triumph of 1952 found neither reason nor reflection in the structure or the life of the Republican Party itself. No aspect or resource of the party . . . could be credited with a vital role in the victory." To friends at the time, he said that Eisenhower "has had to begin with a party so remote from the real-life exercise of responsibility that only one Republican alive in the Senate has ever known the simple experience of serving under a Republican President." These were strong words; they were accurate.

Eisenhower's own attitude to the Republican party was one certainly of scorn, and at times it seemed one almost of loathing, especially of its right wing. Early in 1956, with the impending election in mind, he said to Hughes of the Republican National Committee that it was "All machinery and no imagination. . . . Yes, sir, they can get any Republican elected anywhere in the country—that is, in any solidly Republican district." On another occasion, he exploded with exasperation at "this Simpson"—Richard M. Simpson, a Republican representative from Pennsylvania. "He's spending forty-five thousand dollars a month in charge of congressional campaigns, and he hasn't got a damn Republican elected yet." Speaking the mind of his president, Sherman Adams would retort to the many instent demands that Republican leaders made on Eisenhower: "Nuts! We're doing quite enough for the goddam Republican party." To the end in 1960, the contempt was not qualified.

But it was against the conservative Republicans that Eisenhower's scorn was most brusque. He met the warning that they might dislike his second inaugural address by saying: "I don't give a damn about them. What I try to keep getting across, all the time, is that they don't really speak for the party, so it doesn't matter what noises they make." On another occasion, he exclaimed: "Don't the darn fools realize that the public thinks the dollar sign is the only respected symbol in the Republican Party?" To William Knowland, the right-wing Republican to whom Taft passed on the leadership of the party in the Senate, he said: "I'll support you for governor—but not a damn thing higher than that." In a sweeping denunciation of the whole of the Republican party in Congress, he declared, with a dryness of voice that bit all the more deeply: "I think it's pretty obvious that, when it comes to domestic affairs, the people would rather have the Democrats running things."

It is hardly surprising that such a man should leave the Republican party as lacking in purpose and direction as he had found it. The "very sweep of the Eisenhower victory" in 1952, Emmet John Hughes has said, "left the party still to debate, within itself, its very identity." Both the conservative and the liberal wings could "continue to lay loud claim to being the authentic voices of Republicanism and the hopeful herald of its future." The accuracy of these words can be measured by the fact that at its national convention in 1976 the Republican party was still debating its identity. From time to time, Eisenhower said that his purposes were a "dynamic conservatism," a "progressive moderation," a "moderate progressivism"; and he told a meeting of Republican state chairmen in 1955: "I myself have used such phrases, because we must be known for what we are, the party of progress." He said and did nothing to justify Reinhold Niebuhr's extraordinary judgment that he had "rebuilt American conservatism into a viable political instrument."

The *National Review* was nearer the truth when it said in 1956 that Eisenhower was "personalizing his leadership of the party to the point of blurring beyond distinctive recognition the principles on which Republicanism rests"; and it urged that "we must de-Caesarize Eisenhower," and "infuse a coherent set of principles into the Republican party." Taft had written to Katherine Kennedy Brown, one of the most respected regular leaders of the party, on March 9, 1951, that "if we get Eisenhower we will practically have a Republican New Deal Administration with just as much spending and socialism as under Mr. Truman." Five years later, speaking after the 1956 election; Joseph L. Rauh, Jr., the national chairman of the Americans for Democratic Action, said that Eisenhower had "campaigned on the principles of the New and Fair Deals," and looking at the results in the congressional contests, he added that "In almost every case where a liberal Democrat ran against a conservative Republican for the Senate, the liberal Democrat won." In short, under its personally victorious leader, the Republican party was still at sea.

Eisenhower once said to John Gunther: "If only a man can have courage enough to take the leadership of the middle!" This is exactly the kind of apparently ingenuous statement that one must be guard against in the man. It is too easy to let slide past: Does it not say the obvious? But just as the Democratic party has known for half a century that it must make its appeal from not the center but the left of center, so it is true that the Republican party, if it is to become a securely governing party in the nation, must present its credentials from the right of center.

For a quarter of a century, the myth of the middle has bedeviled the liberal leadership of the Republican party as a result of its refusal to acknowledge that the Eisenhower victories in 1952 and 1956 were not Republican victories. The record of the Republican candidates for Congress, not only in the presidential election years of 1952 and 1956, but also in the midterm elections of 1954 and 1958, was consistently unconvincing. From the eight years of Eisenhower's reign there is no moral for the Republicans to draw. At the end of them, the party had been neither altered nor inspired, least of all had it been straightened, in any essential aspect of its life.

It was characteristic of Eisenhower that when Arthur Larson published *A Republican Looks at His Party,* a book which at once became a bible of "me-tooism" in those years, he appointed Larson to be Under Secretary of Labor; and it was characteristic of them both that, when Larson appeared on *Meet the Press* on August 26, 1956, just as the election campaign was beginning in earnest, he said that the center that the Republicans must hold "includes many Democrats and most Independents." Asked if this center included Adlai Stevenson, who was the rival candidate in the election, Larson answered: "Oh, very definitely." Asked then if it included Dean Acheson, for long a *bête noire* of most Republicans, he replied with the same aplomb: "Oh, yes." Asked then if his own philosophy was also Eisenhower's, Larson did not hesitate: "It's definitely his." What then was the election all about, and one of the exasperated interviewers was heard to mutter: "Maybe we should just flip a coin."

On perhaps no other issue did the Republican rank and file feel more strongly at the time than on the need to maintain the right-to-work legislation that Taft had helped to carry in Congress. But this did not stop Larson from arguing for its repeal. "I think it's an expression of freedom of contract," he said. "If the union and employer exercising ordinary free contract arrive at this kind of [union] contract, I don't think the government should interfere with it. That's a case of the individual . . . having to conform to the will of the majority." This last sentence was uttered in plain defiance of what the Republicans most passionately believed, especially about the nature of private enterprise. A Republican party that could so exalt "the will of the majority" could hardly be perceived to be a Republican party in anything but name.

Larson was not speaking only for himself. Whereas the Democratic platform in that election called for the repeal of the Taft-Hartley Act, the Republican platform over which Eisenhower had absolute control was only a little less straightforward in promising "effective unhindered collective bargaining." Commenting on the Republican platform as a whole, the *National Review* said that the party had "taken unto itself and enlarged" most of the planks of the New Deal and the Fair Deal.

It was the second year in the life of the *National Review,* which became the spokesman and to some extent the symbol of the conservative resentment in the party that Eisenhower, far from doing anything to allay, had instead done much to stimulate. On June 13, 1956, it noticed that the liberal Republican dominance of the Eisenhower administration was "complete and unchallenged," and that the dissent from this dominance was only an undercurrent. But it went on: "The point here is not that the Republican Party is a conservative party: but rather that conservatism has somehow survived within the party, and shows signs of living on long enough to give the liberals some trouble when they no longer have Mr. Eisenhower"—a prophecy that has been roundly fulfilled in the twenty years that have followed. It pointed out that at the Republican Convention that year there had been "important evidence of 'grass-roots' conservatism."

One must give the *National Review* in those early years its full due. It believed in what it believed—returning to the Eisenhower years, one finds oneself speaking like Eisenhower—and it believed in those who believed in what it believed. It saw the true condition of the Republican party at the end of the 1950s with much more clarity than the urbane leaders who believed that somehow they had learned how to occupy the center, that they had proved that they had the courage "to take the leadership of the middle." That the Buckley family should put itself exquisitely at the head of the party's primitives is a curiosity to which we will come, perhaps even a flaw in the conservative position. But at least the conservative spokesmen were nearer the truth than Henry Cabot Lodge when he said that "We are just too damn worried about [the right wing]. . . . Besides, they have nowhere to go but to be with us." They could oust "us," and they did.

There is much to admire in Eisenhower. One cannot help but like a man who, when presented with these words to speak in his first inaugural address: "The world and we have passed the midway point of a century of continuing challenge," scrawled in the margin: "I hate this sentence. *Who challenges whom? What about?"* (Yet one must also note that he uttered the sentence.) His famous "Chance for Peace" speech in 1953 came out of his own inspiration. In the middle of March in that year he had burst out to Emmet John Hughes: "Look, I am tired—and I think everyone is tired—of just plain indictments of the Soviet regime. . . . Instead, just *one* thing matters: what have *we* got to offer the world? What are *we* ready to do, to improve the chances of peace?" John Foster Dulles distrusted the idea of the speech; Winston Churchill thought that the timing of it was wrong: but Eisenhower went ahead and delivered it. "Every gun that is fired, every warship launched, every rocket fired," he said, "signifies in the final sense a theft from those who hunger and are not fed, those who are cold and are not clothed. . . . This is no way of life at all." His attack on the "military-industrial complex" in his farewell address did not spring from a sudden whim.

But the indictment of him as a politician must remain: that he did not effectively lead or educate the party of which he was for eight years the head. Even in foreign policy in which he was mainly interested, he governed for the most part in spite of his party and not with it. Any politician who aspires to the title of statesman, and to exercise a lasting influence on his country, must have a consistently active interest in his party. It must be his primary base for any power and influence that is not merely personal; it alone can provide him with resources beyond those he can personally command; above all, it must be the repository of such ideas and policies as he hopes will survive his own passing from the scene. Eisenhower never thought of the Republican party in these terms.

It may or may not have been right—this is not the point we are arguing—that his administration should have wooed the trade unions, increased social security payments, extended unemployment benefits during a recession, sponsored public housing, and ended with a budget deficit of $12 billion. But a conversion such as this cannot be imposed on a party without causing it to lose any convincing sense of its own identity. It is easy to mock the woman who, after Eisenhower had defeated Taft for the nomination in 1952, walked out of the Hilton Hotel with the lamentation, "This means eight more years of socialism," but in the terms of the political debate of the time she should have claimed, eight years later, this was exactly what the country had got. It makes no sense to say that Eisenhower may not have been a Republican but that he was certainly a conservative, because such conservatism is an unknown quantity until it is forced to define itself within the political context of a party fighting for its electoral survival: pursuing its aims from year to year, and decade to decade, within an environment that, if not always hostile, is usually shifting.

Eisenhower was not interested in the Republican party as it should or might exist after his own regime. His contemptuous attitude to the nomination of Richard Nixon in 1960 only reflected his contemptuous attitude to the party as a whole after 1952.

Referring to the Republican party in private in 1957, he said: "This whole problem of building up men capable of leadership, we've never seemed to meet it the way the British succeed in doing. When their conservatives look around for a leader, they always seem to have two or three men all ready to go." The complaint was justified, but it was a complaint he should have directed as fiercely at himself as at the party. For what did he do in eight years to build the future leadership of the Republicans? If the Conservative party in Britain has in the past always thrown up new and effective leaders when they have been needed, it has in part been because its existing leaders have been deeply involved in the continuing and day-to-day life of the party. Eisenhower had as much interest in the Republican party as an elephant has in an empty peanut shell: with a snort he just blew it aside.

Eisenhower may have been to blame, but not nearly so much as the Eastern and liberal leaders who were responsible, in the first instance, for his nomination, but then made no use of the time he won for them to pull their party together. For we must now turn to the remaining liberal Republicans in our story, who at the national convention in 1976 floated on the tide of events like a school of dead fish, their eyes glazed and their mouths gaping: the soft underbelly, as Churchill would have put it, of the Grand Old Party for more than twenty years.

Men Incapable
of Command

When Caligula made his horse a consul he at least intended it as an affront to the Roman people; the astonishing fact is that, in advancing their names for the presidency of the United States in the past quarter of a century, some of the liberal Republican leaders have believed that they were bestowing an honor.

After all, there is a standard by which they may be judged: the man to whom, as we have seen, many of them cast back their eyes in piety and in emulation, even though in no other respect is it easy to couple the name of Theodore Roosevelt with theirs. We have been told that, one day in 1920, Elihu Root and Henry Stimson were talking in a room where there was a picture of Roosevelt on the wall. At one point, Root looked at it and said: "You know, the more I think over it, the more I feel that Theodore Roosevelt was the greatest teacher of the essential elements of self-government that has ever lived. He was not original, that was not necessary." And of course it is true that Roosevelt saw it one of his functions to be an educator both of his party and of the country; and that in this role he "succeeded in masterful fashion," as E. E. Morrison, the biographer of Stimson, has said, "in stating the nature of the essential problems confronting his society," in spite of the apparent inconsistencies between his often unqualified assertions and his usually limited actions. Partly for this reason, he was for two decades "the makeweight in the dreams of liberal Republicans," and they were shattered by his death. Long after he died, William Allen White recalled the difficulty with which he had tried "to get used to a world without Roosevelt in it," and even later Harold Ickes said that "Something went out of my life that has never been replaced," a remarkable tribute from a man who served an even greater Roosevelt.

These are not the kind of tributes that are likely to be paid to Harold Stassen when at last he passes from the scene: a day which it would be unwise to predict, since those who in the past who have thought to weep to see him "haste away so soon" have always found that the floods that filled their eyes had flowed prematurely. Perhaps the most touching of all the legends on his banners over the years was that of an organization that announced its formation on July 7, 1956, under the name of "Young Americans for Eisenhower First and Stassen Second." That was putting him higher in legend than he has ever been in fact.

One must be hard on Stassen, not because he has been a loser—and a more than ludicrous one at that—but because of the kind of aspirant he has been. He had been elected governor of Minnesota in 1938, when he was in his mid thirties, shortly before his fellow Minnesotan Hubert Humphrey began an equally precocious but more productive career. Humphrey finds it hard to use harsh words about most people in his memoirs, but the few sentences about Stassen that he manages to squeeze on to the paper barely hide their scorn. In 1949, Arthus Schlesinger, Jr., was calling Stassen the leader of "the Young Fogy movement in the Republican Party"; in 1960, the *National Review* awarded him the title of "the dreariest *enfant terrible* of our time." They were saying nothing that Taft had not said privately in 1946, when he described Stassen's thinking as "sophomoric," and complained that he "doesn't know what he is talking about."

But Taft's main complaint was that Stassen only "wraps himself in a mantle of liberalism," while he remained selfish and unreliable. "I may do him an injustice," Taft wrote to David Ingalls, "but I think he is a complete opportunist." Stassen was most ready to flaunt the clothes of the New Deal in the 1940s. In his keynote address to the Republican National Convention on June 24, 1940, he said: "The needs of that portion of our population who have no other means of livelihood shall be met by society as a whole acting through its government." In the *Saturday Evening Post* of May 15, 1943, he proclaimed that "This is not the 1920s," and criticized the Republicans who still wanted to go "back to the old pre-Depression order . . . before social security programs, before strong and legally protected unions, before regulated investment banking." But the same man who could say in 1948 that a "Maginot line type of reactionary thinking will lead just as inevitably to the loss of dynamic economic freedom of men as will the threats from the left" could also proclaim at the same time that the British welfare state and Soviet communism were "two peas from the same confining pod."

Stassen had stepped on to the national scene as an avowed internationalist, but his behavior in December 1942, at the meeting of the Republican National Committee at St. Louis, when Willkie and other internationalist Republicans were trying to keep the party out of isolationist control, was characteristic. As Richard Rovere told the story at the time, Robert McCormick of the Chicago *Tribune* was "moving the constellations" to have Werner W. Schroder, a committeeman from Illinois, elected national chairman of the party. Stassen and his representative, Chris Carlson, a committeewoman from Minnesota, were implored to join the movement to stop Schroder. But although Roy Dunn, the other Minnesota delegate, voted against Schroder, Mrs. Carlson voted for him. As much as anything else, it was this kind of behavior that made his bids for the nomination of his party so futile.

Rovere's judgment in 1944—that "If Stassen is in fact a liberal, his record as a governor offers no more proof than his record in party politics"—was confirmed on the issue of McCarthyism. As early as 1948, during a radio debate on the eve of the Oregon primary, Dewey had said that he thought that the Communist party ought not to be outlawed, but Stassen retorted that this was a "soft policy." In 1951, when Joe McCarthy's attack on the appointment of

Philip Jessup as U.S. representative to the General Assembly of the United Nations was faltering badly, it was Stassen who bolstered the attack, by saying that Jessup was part of a "worldwide pattern of action" by various "Asia hands" who, having sent Chiang Kai-shek to his defeat, were now seeking to do the same to Pandit Nehru. He quoted two meetings in Washington at which Jessup was supposed to have advocated such policies. It was shown that Jessup had not been in Washington at the time of the first meeting, and then that there was no evidence he had taken the position Stassen accused him of taking at the second.

Yet this was the supposedly dedicated internationalist of the postwar years. In the campaign for the Republican nomination in 1952, he slithered all over the place as he agreed to be used by the Eisenhower forces to try to attract delegates from Taft before the convention, but thought that he was using the Eisenhower forces to advance his own delusory chances of the nomination. When he entered the campaign in December 1951, Taft wrote acidly to one Republican senator: "The reporters seem to think he is slightly off beam. Nevertheless, I suppose his very stupidity will lead him to file in various primaries." Even in 1956, when Eisenhower was the incumbent president and a popular candidate, he declared as late as July 9 that "Either the Hon. Earl Warren or I could lead the Republican Party to victory over Adlai Stevenson." In these crucial years, when the Republican party might have been effectively rebuilt, Stassen showed no interest in the task. Taft in 1952 tried to build bridges to him, but his efforts were only rebuffed.

In 1964 Stassen still entered his name in the lists, but by now the joke was thin. As the other liberal Republicans went down to ignominious defeat before Barry Goldwater, the chairman of the Democratic National Committee, John Bailey, said that "Their only chance of fame is if they are drafted as the stop-Stassen candidates." In 1968 he again entered the campaign for the nomination, as a "peace" candidate on the issue of the Vietnam War, this dedicated internationalist who in the previous decade had accused the men in Washington of wishing to treat with the communist world. Even his failures were lacking in honor.

Once again we must realize that our scorn is not for his

failure as such, nor even for the fact that he may all along have been "slightly off beam." There have been many losers in history who have been noble and even strong, whose lives we find inspiring. But although something can be said for winning with dishonor, there is nothing to be said for losing with dishonor. Such as it has been, his career has been shabby, since as the young Republican governor of Minnesota he made a deal with the local leadership of the International Teamsters Union, careless of principle, and heedless of the welfare of his party. Moreover, the point is that in much of his behavior he has not been aberrant, but only representative of the very liberal Republicans we are describing, in whom (lack of) political character is joined to (lack of) political principle.

It is more difficult to be hard on William Scranton. He had little experience of national politics when he ran for the Republican nomination in 1964, and in fact he appears to have had no real personal ambition to run for it at all. He has all the attributes of a lightweight: "six foot two of lean American man," as Theodore White has said, with that gift for rhapsody in his writing\that one always hopes (but is never sure) he intends as irony, "the body slender and muscular from skiing in winter, tennis in summer. From Washington, Pa., to Washington, D.C., when William Warren Scranton moves through the room, the eyes of dowagers caress him as a son, and young girls wriggle." When he presented his combined message on the budget and the state of the commonwealth to the Pennsylvania legislature in 1964, he spoke for half an hour without drawing any applause, and it was dryly observed at the time that some of the Pennsylvania leaders of the Republican party hoped that in the following year he would run as the son from another state.

But it cannot quite be left there. After he delivered this message, the leader of the Democrats in Pennsylvania, Anthony J. Presky, said that he was "happy that the Governor has embraced the thinking of the Democratic Party in several areas of the state government." It was again this "me-tooism" of the liberal Republicans, whenever they were returned to office, that disturbed the conservative rank and file of the party. A delegate from a rural area of Pennsylvania to the Republican Convention in 1964 said that he admired Goldwater, not only because he agreed with "his philosophies of government" but even more for his "moral integrity. I have always believed that a candidate should carry out his promises. Scranton didn't do that." The primitives in a party may require too much of the wrong kind of "moral integrity" from their politicians —politics demands some adjustment to political realities —but the fact remains that the liberal Republicans have persistently refused to acknowledge that the policies which they pursue must bear at least some tenuous relationship to the principles for which their party is supposed to stand.

"Through the great part of its history, through the greatest of its successes, the Republican Party served America not by standing as the negative party but by serving as the party of positive accomplishment." So Scranton spoke in a closed-circuit television address to a series of Republican fund-raising dinners on January 29, 1964. There at least was something of the voice of Theodore Roosevelt; but how hollow it now sounded from the son of the "Duchess," as his mother, Mrs. Worthington Scranton, was popularly known. And how hollow the same voice sounded from all of the liberal Republicans who were put forward in the 1960s as men who could hold back the rising tide of conservatism in their party.

By 1967, with Goldwater out of the way and Reagan still to arrive, the list of the liberals seemed long and promising. Apart from Scranton, was there not Charles Percy, the senator from Illinois; George Romney, the governor of Michigan; Nelson Rockefeller, the governor of New York; Jacob Javits, the senator from New York; John V. Lindsay, the mayor of New York; John Volpe, the governor of Massachusetts; Edward Brooke, the senator from Massachusetts; Thruston Morton, the senator from Kentucky; Mark Hatfield, the senator from Oregon; John Chafee, the governor of Rhode Island; Daniel Evans, the governor of Washington; and who else could not be counted? Men of mettle, all of them, the country was told, whose answer to the conservatives in their party would be that of Pétain at Verdun: "They shall not pass."

But where were they in the next ten years, where are they now, where they could be seen at the Republican Convention in 1976, except in the shadows? In years that were critical to their party, they seemed incapable of standing either alone or together, as the conservatives prepared to storm even its inner fastnesses.

What is one to say of George Romney, who retreated even before he had set foot on the bridge he was meant to defend? He announced his withdrawal from the campaign for the Republican nomination less than two weeks before the primary in New Hampshire. He blamed his destruction on the press—"I think that the press has been very negative for a long time toward me. There isn't any doubt about that"—but the press can do only so much in tripping up a politician, if the politician does not help it. It was Romney himself who went in search of national exposure and who, in doing so, placed the rocks in his own path, walked back two or three paces in order then to negotiate them more comfortably, and at once fell flat on his face over each of them. A candidate who says that he can be "brainwashed" on an issue as searching as Vietnam is a candidate of whom not only the press but the electors are likely to ask how much brain there was in the first place.

And what is one to say of Charles Percy, whose nickname of "Chuck" was translated into "Chuckles" almost as soon as he arrived in Washington, a diminutive that seemed irresistibly appropriate to his heavy but implausible gravity. His opponent in Illinois, Paul Douglas, said that Percy had raised vacillation to the level of a moral principle. He was at one moment against open occupancy laws, he was then for them; at one moment against reapportionment and then for it. His comment on Eisenhower deserves to be savored: "For the time in which he served, General Eisenhower was a very great man. But he didn't get my daughter to go to Africa; John Kennedy did that." It is hard to believe that Percy has got anyone in Illinois to go even as far as round the block to buy a thumbtack.

Studiously promoting his reputation as a moderate liberal, he met the nomination of Goldwater in 1964 by giving the proclaimed enemy of moderation at least his moderate support. He rolled with the Goldwater tide, one observer said. But there are storms in which to roll with the tide is no guarantee that one will not ship a lot of water. Percy shipped enough water in 1964 to sink even a serious liberal reputation; his own was already so fragile that it evaporated.

And where now is John Lindsay, who scuttled from his party in what must surely have been one of the most ill-considered acts of political desperation of which any politician could be capable? He must be somewhere if one could think where to look for him; but what would one do with him if one found him? And whatever happened to Mark Hatfield, who was once pleased to proclaim himself the "Rockefeller of the West," a sobriquet which a more circumspect man would anyhow have disdained, and that even he abandoned when Rockefeller announced his divorce and his remarriage? And what really is Elliott Richardson, a man whose center sometimes seems to be so soft that one almost thinks it must have been of him that Yeats wrote that "the center cannot hold"? He has occupied an almost unseemly number of government posts, and drawn from this experience no advice for his party that ever compels its attention.

One follows the list, from once bright name to now di-shevelled career, and is dumbfounded. For it is not the individual characters of the men that is of most interest, but the political character of a breed. There must be something wrong with these heirs of a political tradition of whom Theodore Roosevelt might well have said, as Wellington said of the British troops at Waterloo: "I don't know what they do to the enemy, but by God they frighten me!"

So one turns to the most lackluster of them all: to the man who throughout the whole period has been perhaps the most ineffably incompetent politician on the national scene, the All Star of Born Losers, the black hole of the Republican universe into which astronomers gaze wondering if there can be such a thing as absolute nothingness, the leader who did not have to be buried in 1976 because he had self-destructed so often, the most dishevelled of them all, Nelson Rockefeller. It appears from the first pictures from Mars that there is no life on the planet: not in the sense of someone like a person walking about its surface. But we must consider that if a spacecraft landed on our own Earth and showed pictures only of Nelson Rockefeller, we might not recognize it as life. If in an earlier age his disembowelment had been ordered, he would probably at once have been declared a saint by his bewildered torturers when they discovered that from this man who had walked and breathed there was not even a length of gut to be extracted: that within this life there had been only a space.

If these words seem harsh, he has earned them. He has enjoyed the advantages of great wealth; both socially and politically he has been in a position of great influence; for a long time he has held in his hands the instruments of great power. If the failure of the liberal Republicans has a prototype, it can best be found in him.

The three crucial elections at which the liberal Republicans might have hoped that Rockefeller would move effectively to contain the conservatives and pull the party together were all in the 1960s: at the first, the victory inside the party went to Nixon; at the second, to Goldwater; at the third it went once more to Nixon. In each of the campaigns for the nomination, Rockefeller was indecisive; his vacillations undermined the liberal hopes, and ultimately they were arrogant. He wished to be given the nomination, not to have to work for it.

On November 16, 1960, *Time* reported in the breathless style its rewrite men then used: "Nelson Rockefeller quivered on his launching pad, preparing to take off this week on a breathtaking 'non-political' swoosh through California and three other Western states. In Albany, meanwhile, Rocky was assembling a high-octane, Presidential-type staff of experts." But a month later he withdrew—this was the year in which he excused his decision not to run in the primaries on the ground that he could not find the money—and the *National Review* poured out a justified scorn: "A slick, big-moneyed, high-liberal operation collapsed . . . with all his resources, with all his speech-writers, with a million grins for a million people, with his political loftiness and his economic paternalism, and the support from liberal fortresses"; the man who a month before had been "quivering on his launching pad" simply did not take off. He was a dud.

January went by; February ran its twenty-nine days; March gave way to April; and then May to June: and all the time, in the absence of a liberal candidate of any stature, Nixon built his strength for the Republican Convention. Then all at once, Rockefeller announced that, although he had not been a candidate in the primaries, he would be one at the convention. He said that he had held back his announcement until then because he did not wish to embarrass the Eisenhower administration before the summit conference, a plea which took in no one. But he was now compelled to speak out bluntly because Nixon had "firmly insisted upon making known his program and his policies not before, but only after nomination by his party."

This was gall enough, since Nixon had spoken at forty-seven press conferences and forums in the previous five months, and could reasonably claim, as he did, that he had "set forth with greater precision and more detail my views on the major issues than any" of the other candidates. But the gall was unbelievable when he went on to describe Nixon as a candidate "whose only emblem is a question mark," and to say that "the path of great leadership does not lie along the top of a fence." This from the man whose candidacy had been only a question mark and who had sat for so long on the fence that the rust seemed to have entered his mind. He was a candidate for a draft, but he would toil not, neither would he spin.

In the spring of 1963, the Eastern and liberal leaders of the party, unaware of what was already being engineered among the grassroots by the promoters of Barry Goldwater, were certain that Rockefeller would be nominated. But on May 4, it was announced that he had married Mrs. Margaretta "Happy" Murphy, and one of the leaders summed up the consequences: "Rocky's got the best delegate hunters in the country. But with this re-marriage, all they can do is sit up there on the fifty-sixth floor of the Rockefeller Center." One thing was clear: Rockefeller this time had to enter and win some primaries, and win them early.

But the efforts of the liberal leadership were divided. In New Hampshire a write-in vote for Henry Cabot Lodge gave him the lead over both Goldwater and Rockefeller. As late as the Oregon primary, on which Rockefeller spent $460,000 (as compared with $54,000 spent by Lodge), Rockefeller could still gain only a small lead over Lodge. Nevertheless this result was enough to end Lodge's chances, and his supporters in the crucial California primary advised the voters to support Rockefeller, a move

that William Scranton described as "moral and logical."
Rockefeller campaigned strongly—it was here that he
created the issues of social security and nuclear war that
the Democrats were later to use against Goldwater—but
it was too late. The response of Goldwater's supporters
was to call into action the precinct organizations they had
been building so carefully: Rockefeller was overwhelmed,
and Goldwater assured of a first-ballot nomination.

The story is pathetic because Rockefeller and the liberal leadership of the Republican party had had four
years, since the defeat of Nixon in 1960, to establish their
command. Rockefeller himself had begun to build his
campaign immediately after the Republican Convention
in 1960: there was no pretense this time that he could
not find the money, and was not willing to spend it. Yet
in the first primary in New Hampshire, the liberal forces
were divided (Lodge 25.5 percent, Goldwater 23.2 percent, Rockefeller 21.0 percent); although the positions in
Oregon were changed (Rockefeller 33 percent, Lodge
28 percent, Goldwater 17 percent), the division was as
deep as ever; and as the California primary campaign began in earnest, Lodge was still leading Rockefeller by 33
percent to 10 percent in the public opinion polls. If
Rockefeller was to have any chance of winning in these
circumstances, he had to strangle the Lodge campaign
early in the year or make a deal with an opponent who
was not even in the country; characteristically he did
neither.

By the end of April that year, Goldwater had already
accumulated more than five hundred delegates, and one
of the Eastern and liberal leaders of the party said that if
he was to be stopped it was essential that Lodge should
return home from Saigon; but Lodge refused, and as
much blame for the 1964 debacle must rest on him as on
Rockefeller. He ought either to have called off his supporters or come home to win the primary campaigns; he
did neither. So two of the most substantial figures of the
urbane leadership of the party fought each other into the
ground, and threw the nomination to the primitives.

The story in 1968 was no better. At the beginning of
the year, almost every significant Republican leader was
urging Rockefeller to enter the primaries in order to hold
off the threat from an unexpectedly resurgent Nixon, but

Rockefeller stuck to his announced position that he was a supporter of George Romney. He stuck to it, that is, but modified it. Less than a month before the New Hampshire primary, he said that he would consider a draft for the nomination if he were presented with one at the convention itself: "I could not avoid it." He was up to his old tricks, and Melvin Laird, who was at the time one of his strong supporters, retorted that if Rockefeller did not become an active candidate, "I don't believe he can be drafted." Even if Romney had had any chance in New Hampshire, Rockefeller had pulled the ground from under him; but when Romney withdrew from the campaign even before New Hampshire, Rockefeller said only that he was "ready and willing" to run for the nomination, "if called." In the circumstances such a statement was fatuous: He was being called by almost the entire leadership of a party that dreaded the thought of Richard Nixon. The Republican party's fear of Nixon is too often forgotten. It did not want him.

Tom McCall, the governor of Oregon and one of the most vigorous supporters of Rockefeller, said that he was "flabbergasted that Rockefeller said let's play it cool. . . . Rockefeller no longer has any reason for not being in. This is where he ought to make his stand." This was like calling on a jellyfish to stand upright. On March 10, thirty-one important Republican leaders met Rockefeller at his Manhattan apartment and urged him to enter the campaign. Eleven days later, the response of Rockefeller was that he would not seek the nomination but would accept a draft from the national convention. On April 1, after Lyndon Johnson had announced his withdrawal from the campaign, Rockefeller said of his own intentions: "I am a great believer in waiting and absorbing the impact of what's going on." By April 10, he had absorbed, and announced that he was "available" for the nomination: "Availability is the way I'd put it, rather than an active candidacy." And with that he went out, absorbent as a paper towel, to spend $7 million trying to impress the Republican delegates not with his ability as a campaigner but with his strength in the public opinion polls.

The effort was fruitless. Nixon was nominated and elected in 1968; renominated and reelected in 1972; forced to resign and succeeded by a conservative in 1974;

and by 1976, at the Republican Convention in Kansas City, the liberals were in disarray and neglected, and Rockefeller himself was happy to be patted on the knee by Walter Cronkite.

There are men in public life who deserve to be dismissed with scorn, as Tocqueville dismissed the French politicians who in 1848 could not, until the eve of the revolution of that year, see what was happening under their noses. "The real cause, the effective one, that makes men lose power," he said in a speech in the Chamber of Deputies on January 29, 1848, "is that they have become unworthy to exercise it . . . incapable and unworthy of ruling." This is the indictment that must be made of the liberal Republicans in general, and of Nelson Rockefeller in particular. Year after year, for nearly half a century, election after election, they have proved themselves unfit, either to command their party or to govern their country; least of all to deserve the trust of the people.

They have not known what they wanted, cared enough to fight for it, had either the aptness or the courage to command it. They have conceded when they ought to have struggled; capitulated when they might have had victory; fought only when they have already engineered their own defeat. They have been indifferent to opportunities, selfish in purpose, confined in vision, feeble in action, insensible to danger: trifling men who could not meet the challenge of their own times.

The Rage Against the East

WE ARE TRYNG TO find out what the Republican party is in order then to understand less why it is still so distrusted by the people than why it is so distrusted by itself; even unknown to itself, and so unknown to others. Parties are beasts: we should be able to imagine and to describe them like the animals, real or legendary, in a bestiary. But it is exactly this which it is difficult to do with the Republican party. One might say that there is nothing heraldic about; it does not blazon itself on our consciousnesses, or on that of the country; it is not *passant,* or *rampant* or even *couchant.* Although of little brain, the elephant is an imposing animal, but one looks at this elephant, and all one is reminded of is Dumbo, and even Dumbo had ears that spread like wings.

One way to approach the subject is to try to understand why the conservative Republicans have for so long been so ferocious in their denunciations of the influence of the "East" or the "Eastern Establishment" or "New York" or "Wall Street" on the conventional leadership of the party. After all, one would expect a conservative Republican to approve of Wall Street, indeed to see it as one of his functions to defend Wall Street. But it is not so; he detests the very interest his party exists (to some extent) to serve.

It is worth realizing that the attack from within the Republican party on what we now call the "Eastern Establishment" came long before Goldwater suggested that the eastern seaboard should be sawn off and floated out to sea—by far the liveliest of his proposals—and one that struck a chord in not only Republican breasts from the Mississippi to the Pacific and from the Mason-Dixon line to the Gulf. The "Eastern Establishment" was bitterly denounced, from early in his career until the end of it, by Robert Taft, perhaps the most important Republican leader, both in his successes and in his defeats, since Theodore Roosevelt. The title of "Mr. Republican" was not given to him falsely or thoughtlessly.

Taft was of course a midwesterner, and as early as 1928, after the election of Hoover, he wrote a letter to his father in which his bitterness against the East as such, although in this case the East as represented by the forces of Al Smith, was spat out: "I am looking forward to reading *Life, Time,* the *Nation,* and the *New Republic,* and seeing how they take the result. The discomfiture of the Eastern intelligentsia gives me as much pleasure as that of the radical farm leaders," by which he meant the remnants of the Progressives. A man who, even in 1928, could lump *Life* and *Time* together with the *Nation* and the *New Republic* was creating a symbol of something he feared or hated, or both: of something real to him.

By the time he first ran for the nomination of his party in 1940, to be defeated by Willkie, he accurately enough fixed part of the credit for Willkie's victory on the way he had been sponsored by the "Eastern Establishment." "More than ever," says his excellent biographer, James T. Patterson, "he [Taft] suspected Wall Street financiers, syndicated columnists, mass circulation magazines, and Eastern intellectuals." He was not alone. In 1940 also, Senator Gerald P. Nye, of North Dakota, spoke darkly of the Eastern forces he said were raising huge sums of money to defeat him. The list is familiar to us today. Goldwater in 1964 and Reagan to a lesser extent in 1972 marked out the same obstructers of their march to power: the financiers, the columnists, the press, the intellectuals, all of the East.

In 1944 Taft renewed his complaint. As Dewey took an insurmountable lead in the struggle for the nomination, he wrote to a friend that Dewey "comes from New York and sees the group opinions there as much more important than they are." As his biographer again says, "Taft's instinctive distrust of Eastern Republicans . . . was rising uncontrollably to the surface," and in 1944 as in 1940, it merely seemed to him that "a New Yorker representing the Eastern wing of the party had triumphed over the stalwarts from Ohio." No legacy of Taft to his party was more important than this geographical definition of an ideological difference.

His complaints had a justification. Both in 1944 and in 1948 Dewey relied almost exclusively on advisors from New York State and in the Eastern Establishment; he seemed almost to be willing to throw away the rest of the country. On June 29, 1948, after Dewey had been nominated, Taft wrote to Dwight Green, the governor of Illinois: "I urged your name on Tom Dewey [for the vice-presidential nomination] but I got little response except that you were too closely connected with the Chicago *Tribune*. Tom's whole concern seemed to be about carrying the Atlantic, and he seemed to be afraid of all Midwestern candidates because they were too 'isolationist.' " On the same day, he wrote to Katharine Kennedy Brown, a long-established member of the Republican National Committee: "I am chiefly afraid that he will pay too much attention to the Eastern newspapers, which seem to have created a lot of wholly false issues": issues that were used, he meant, to set some Republicans beyond the pale.

In 1952 his struggle against the Eastern influence in his party culminated in his head-on collision with the forces that nominated Eisenhower. The same businessmen in the East who had helped Willkie against Taft and Arthur Vandenberg in 1940, and thrown themselves behind Dewey in 1944 and 1948, were now rounded up by Dewey behind the general. As he went down to defeat, Taft wrote to his friends that "the main Eisenhower men seem to be the international bankers, the Dewey organization allied with them, the Republican New Dealers, and even President Truman. Apparently they wish to be sure that, no matter which party wins, they win." And again: "My greatest handicap in this whole campaign has been the solid backing of General Eisenhower by many of the Eastern papers and others throughout the country as well as a majority of the national magazines, syndicated columnists and commentators."

Over twelve years, and in four campaigns for the nomination of his party, Taft saw the enemy, and it was them. If it was not he who drew the line of the rift which has divided the Republican party ever since—it was bleakly noticeable in the delegate votes cast for Gerald Ford and Ronald Reagan in 1976—he certainly helped to mark it on the political map in the imagination of the party's members and its leaders.

By the 1960s, seven years after Taft's death, Goldwater and his supporters were in full cry against the Eastern Establishment. Some of the attacks were savage. L. Brent Bozell wrote in the *National Review* in 1960 that "the Republican Party is controlled by the kind of people who would rather win with anybody than lose with somebody congenial. Such people tend to live in the East. Some of them represent financial interests with peculiar reasons for wanting victory for victory's sake. Others are politicians, and in the East the GOP politician tends to be more pragmatic and less ideological than his counterpart in the Midwest and West."

Four years later, when Goldwater announced his candidacy, the *National Review* hailed him as "a Republican politician who aspires to the Presidency and does not first shrive himself in the waters of Wall Street. . . . He durst not resist the call which was heard right over the potent voices of the Eastern curia, [from Americans] asking primarily for their own emancipation from the decadent East." Rockefeller was denounced as the nominee of "the Eastern kingmakers," and he himself as "the manicured Eastern plutocrat." This is lusty language, but one may say in passing that the image it creates—of the Buckley family at the *National Review,* with unclean nails, the spokesmen of the sans-culottes—is affecting even if unexpected.

For forty years the battle against the East—the very East where much of its strength used to lie—has raged within the Republican party, consuming its energy and even paralyzing it. This must tell us something of the nature of the beast.

That there are differences of interest between various regions of the country does not really explain the division in the Republican party, and especially the antagonism of the conservatives to the East. Politics is a perpetual adjustment of interests, whatever else it may be; and if interests that appear to conflict were irreconcilable, Franklin Roosevelt could never have held the South and the North, the cities and the farmers, together in the coalition he created. Too much is made today of a supposed conflict of interests between a "new" Southwest and South and the "old" East. One has to look only at Houston, as booming a city as any in America, an industrial and commercial center of exceptional and still growing prosperity, to realize that it is not yet (as distinct from the industrial and commercial) base of its prosperity it still looks to New York. There is no financial center in the Sun Belt, from Atlanta to Phoenix; and even the state of California, which industrially and commercially is almost like a sovereign nation, cannot boast a true financial center.

Moreover, if this is true of the huge private investment the Sun Belt requires, it is no less true of the public investment it needs from the federal government. In terms of their own development, the South and the Southwest today cannot do without Washington any more than they can do without Wall Street. Many Republicans were surprised at the strong sentiment that was displayed across the country in 1975 in favor of "bailing out" New York. But this sentiment grew out of not merely a natural regard for the city, which is in many ways one of the most potent symbols of America, the gateway through which the immigrants came to the New World, but also an appreciation of how much the rest of the nation still depends on New York. Equally, the federal government in Washington does proportionately more for the South and the Southwest than for any other regions. If interests were all that counted in politics the East would not be so symbolic an enemy to so many people.

This does not mean that there are no differences of interest. However small the percentage of the population that is now engaged directly in agriculture, the Midwest still perceives itself as a farming Midwest, certainly as *non-metropolitan* in interest and spirit, even in its cities.

The complaint Taft made against the East after the 1948 election is still echoed in the Midwest thirty years later: that Dewey "lost in the rural districts," and that he lost because "the farmers felt that Truman had done a fairly good job for them, and that Dewey had no sympathy whatever for the farm position." Equally, it was as early as 1952 that some observers noted there was in the Southwest a new breed of millionaires and would-be millionaires among the contributors to the Republican party who "seemed to want little more than freedom from governmental restraint," while the great wealth of the East had since 1932 made its deal with the government.

But neither these differences, nor any others, account for the persistence of the geographical division in the party; not only its persistence, but also its bitterness. A list of the delegate votes from the various states Eisenhower and Taft took with them to the Republican National Convention in 1952 reads very like the list of the delegate support on which Ford and Reagan could rely almost a quarter of a century later. Something more than interests, real or perceived, is at work here.

The fear many people have of the East, and which is given voice by the conservative Republicans, is not so much an alarm for their own interests, or the interests that they represent, as for their perceptions of the modern world, and of their own place in it. The kind of patriotism that finds expression west of the Mississippi and south of the Mason-Dixon line rests on a belief in the exceptionalism of America, in its "exemption from history," especially from the history of Europe. The phrase "the eastern seaboard" springs naturally to the lips of men like Barry Goldwater, because it is an *Atlantic* seaboard; and if floated out to sea, it would drift naturally back across the ocean and attach itself to Europe again. In the Americans who feel threatened by the East, one finds a rejection of the "fear and failure" that now lie at the heart of the Old World: a conviction that America began anew, and that it may still again begin anew, if that is necessary to recover its original inspiration.

When in his speech to the Republican National Convention in 1968 Goldwater drew his imagery from his own state, and seemed to plead for a desert to sweep across the nation and cleanse it, he was raising a hope of the renewal and reinvigoration of American exceptionalism to which many Americans still respond.

One senses this vividly in the isolationism of Robert Taft. He was quickly and deeply disillusioned by the quarrelsomeness of the European nations after the First World War, when he worked on Herbert Hoover's agency to distribute relief to the war-torn continent; and this impression never left him. On October 13, 1919, he wrote: "European quarrels are everlasting. There is a welter of races there so confused that boundaries cannot be drawn without leaving minorities which are a perpetual source of friction." In a speech as late as September 22, 1941, he said: "If isolationism means isolation from European wars, I am an isolationist." Foreign nations were simply incomprehensible. In April 1947 a writer in *Fortune* remarked that to Taft "other countries seem merely odd places, full of uncertain plumbing, funny-colored money, and people talking languages one can't understand." It was not really a caricature.

In fact, many thought that his isolationism merely reflected his irritation with having to be concerned with foreign affairs at all. On November 25, 1941, he wrote to a friend: "Nine years out of ten, the fundamental issue is one of domestic policy, and we ought not to permit the breaking up of a party on any question of foreign policy." Yet his own adamant opposition to American intervention abroad—which appears to have included, according to a paper found after his death, opposition to intervention in Indochina—was itself a cause of deep division within the Republican party for one and a half decades.

Since the Second World War, the isolationism of the right wing has undergone a mutation into as ardent an interventionism, but the motives are the same: a suspicion of the rest of the world, an impatience with its complexities, and a desire for solutions that are simple. In this situation, the internationalism of the Eastern Establishment is the same and as objectionable as it was before. The "international bankers" and the "Establishment," and even something as vague as "big business," will do almost anything, according to the suspicions of the conservatives, to sustain their financial and trading interests:

will traduce and betray, not only exceptional American interests, but an exceptional American faith, if the account books justify it.

It would have come as no surprise to the conservatives to know that Charles Wilson, the defense secretary in Eisenhower's administration, had asked in Cabinet: "Is there no possibility for a package deal [over Korea]? Maybe we could recognize Red China, and get the Far East settled." All that the conservatives believe to be immoral in big business and Wall Street is summed up in the casualness of that proposal, just as they were shocked twenty years later when Richard Nixon, with the support of the Eastern Establishment, did indeed seek a rapprochement with communist China. The East in this view is not only immoral, it is immoral in part because it is decadent, and this decadence is a taint from the Old World.

When a midwesterner such as William Allen White—a Republican but by no means a conservative—spoke of "the detachment of Groton and Harvard . . . the suavity of Lawrenceville and Princeton . . . the smugness of Hotchkiss and Yale," he was talking not only of manners but of certain attitudes in the East that are too ready to make political adjustments at the expense of moral commitment, and too sure that the world can be managed by its own finesse. As a conservative Republican once said to an inquirer in Fredericksburg, Texas: "I think that what many of us feel about the East is that it is frightened to be accused of naïveté."

But from the beginning of our story, creating in him responses which still echo today, the conservative Republican has been just as much disturbed by the acquiescence of the Eastern Establishment or Wall Street in if not every measure of the New Deal at least its general propositions. Earl Warren was thus regarded as a spokesman of the Eastern and liberal leadership, even before he became the chief justice of the Supreme Court, and handed down the unanimous decision in *Brown* vs. *Board of Education*. "It is hard for me to see," Taft wrote to a friend on December 27, 1950, "how any real Republicans could be for Warren today. He certainly represents all the New Deal principles, and does not even recognize that there is any difference in principle." The "lack of courage" that

Taft found in Dewey lay precisely in Dewey's refusal to define clearly the ground of principle on which the Republican party was and, he would have said, must be opposed to the New Deal.

As in foreign policy, the conservative appealed against the Eastern Establishment to an American exceptionalism. "The measures undertaken by the Democratic Administration are alarming," Taft wrote in a letter on February 2, 1934. "Whatever may be said for them as emergency measures, their permanent incorporation into our system could practically abandon the whole theory of American government." What mattered in this theory was to be found in the Declaration of Independence. "It is somewhat significant," he said in 1939, "that the right endowed is not one of happiness but merely of pursuit. . . . The whole history of America reveals a system based on individual opportunity, individual initiative, individual freedom to earn one's own living in one's own way, and to conduct manufacturing, commerce, agriculture, or other business, on rugged individualism, if you please, which it has become so fashionable to deride."

Taft's famous remark in 1936, which was to haunt him for the rest of his life—that he believed that "thrift, industry, and intelligence produce happiness today as they produced it in the horse-and-buggy days"—must be taken seriously. Again there was the emphasis on happiness as an individual pursuit; and the American is particularly endowed with the right to that pursuit by his circumstances, his theory of government, and his history. This may be naïve; it is not nonsense. It is an American belief in which, many Americans think, the East has become disillusioned. The movement toward totalitarianism that Taft saw in the New Deal was a movement *back in time* to an Old World sickness, from which America had escaped (or had given itself the opportunity to escape) when it exempted itself from history, and the East is too close to the Old World, too infected with its fear and failure, to claim this exemption.

This nostalgia for "the horse-and-buggy days," however much we may question it later, is also something other and more important than mere nostalgia. It represents a stance from which the modern world may be criticized and even "made over." There are two kinds of revolutionaries against the world as it now is: those on the left who revolt against it in favor of an imagined utopia in the future, and those on the right who revolt against it in favor of an imagined golden age in the past. The affection for "the horse-and-buggy days" is just such a revolt, and it is from this position that the conservative west of the Mississippi makes his criticism, today as much as ever, of the liberal in the East.

At the Republican Convention in 1944, I. F. Stone described the supporters of John Bricker, the governor of Ohio, "with their boys' choirs, lady cellist, and hymns . . . Bricker's [girls] were soulful young things." But it is equally true that twenty years later one could gaze on the supporters of Barry Goldwater, and thirty years later on those of Ronald Reagan, and see, with only superficial changes in dress and manners, the same people.

The young supporters of Goldwater and Reagan—from the Midwest, the West, and the Southwest—are still "soulful young things." As someone has said of Huckleberry Finn, the nostalgia for a lost childhood that is depicted in him is particularly American in that it is not so much a nostalgia for a lost past as a nostalgia for a lost future. The indifference of the Eastern liberal to the meaning of this nostalgia for a "lost future" accounts as much as anything else for his own undoing in the Republican party, but also for the geographical lines along which for almost forty years its ideological divisions have been drawn.

Not only did the contest between Ford and Reagan for the nomination in 1976 vividly demonstrate the depth of this geographical division, but the results of the election then confirmed it: the line drawn across the country from north to south, separating with only a few exceptions the states that voted for Ford from those that voted for Carter. Apart from the question whether the Republican party can be satisfied with a political base that is generally weak in electoral votes, a more difficult question is raised: whether in the twentieth century a party that is so influenced by a belief in American exceptionalism drawn from "the horse-and-buggy days" can be a party that lives in its own time.

The Making of a Conservative

ROBERT TAFT MATTERS. BECAUSE he never reached the White House, it is hard to say that he is as important to the Republican party in this century as Franklin Roosevelt has been to the Democratic party. He is not now celebrated by Republicans as Roosevelt is still celebrated by Democrats; his is not today a name to conjure with. The liberal Republicans who disdained and defeated him while he was alive do not dare to raise his ghost; even the conservative Republicans have been careless of some of the most important of his teachings. Yet in no Republican in the past half-century has political character (and not the lack of it) been so joined to political principle (and not the lack of it). Not to know of Taft—not to let him into one's mind, into one's very bones, even if it is only then to expel him—is not to live and breathe the politics of America in this century, and not to have one's being in it.

Almost every account of Taft pays tribute to his honor, and this is interesting: The tributes are not casual, any more than are the similar tributes to Goldwater. Yet when all is said, the more telling phrase is that of Hubert Humphrey: that Taft "had a kind of integrity"; and he proceeds to speak of this integrity in terms of Taft's political tenacity—his stubbornness and his perseverance. This is a valuable correction—or modification—of the general tributes, and sheds some light on the supposition, which has gained a lot of ground in recent years, that the conservative Republican is a man of exceptional honor in a time of political expediency and deviousness: that he is pure, that he is sincere, that he does not go back on his promises, all of which could be said of Hitler, perhaps the most sincere man in the political life of this century, who said what he would do, believed that it should be done, and did it without a qualm. Political honor is not to be described or measured in the same terms as personal honor.

One cannot help admiring a man who in 1940, on the first occasion that he envisaged trying for the presidential nomination, refused to alter his views on foreign policy, even though Hitler was overrunning the whole of the European continent. In Kansas in that year, Turner Catledge of the *New York Times* came across Taft in a Pullman car: "His glasses had slipped down, halfway off his face, and he kept repeating, in a distant voice, 'I'm just not going to do it.'" Thirty years later, Catledge said in his memoirs that Taft "couldn't shift his views for political expedience, and that was one reason why he never captured the Republican nomination." Well, yes! but also no!—as we shall see.

At about the same time in 1940, Taft was invited to dinner by Ogden Reid, the publisher, and found that the other guests were all representatives of the Eastern Establishment who favored giving more and immediate aid to the allies who were fighting Hitler. At last, according to his wife, Taft "exploded with a loud pop. Said he: 'I had not intended to take any part in this discussion but I feel that I cannot sit here and let my silence be interpreted as agreement.' Then the fat was in the fire"; the argument was angry, and it would not be too much to say that, by his interruption at that dinner, Taft forfeited the support of the Eastern Establishment for the rest of his career.

There is something to admire in it—of course there is —as long as one realizes that if Taft (or anyone else) had said that Hitler, by overrunning the continent, had so altered the circumstances that it had also altered his opinion of what was necessary, he would have been no less honorable. To be adamant in the face of events may be proof of a kind of integrity or *only* of a kind of stubbornness, of a kind of courage or *only* of a kind of insularity.

There is something to admire also in Taft's disdain for some of the new methods of politics. He resisted the tendency of "newspapers, magazines, and columnists, to regard politics as a show in which only an actor can be promoted. This state of mind," he wrote to a friend, "affected all of the leaders who really should have been for me." He once said to a journalist, "The trouble with glamour is what's so frequently underneath it"; and when the journalist asked him what that was, Taft replied: "Too little." Again one can admire it, but one must at the same time remember that Taft's appearance and character and temperament were not easy to "glamorize," that he had a motive for his disdain. He himself hired public relations firms to "humanize" and project his image. He was prepared to use the methods; they were simply not appropriate for him.

In fact, much of his "kind of integrity" was a reflection not only of a stubbornness that degenerated often into irritability but also of a dogmatism that may have some justification and even function in the ideologue, but has very little of either in the politician. Richard Rovere wrote of few politicians at the time either so well or with so much sympathy as he wrote of Taft, whom he described as "unique, identifiable, typical of himself," adding that it was for this reason that he "died a Senator who will be remembered," a salute that has stood the test of time. But he also observed that Taft was "an odd, improbable combination of sweet reasonableness and ungovernable passion."

It is at this point that one must recognize that his "kind of integrity," although it is not to be denied, is also a reflection of something else. For a reasonable man, and it was as such that he would have liked to have been perceived, he was often given to bewildering exaggeration. Of the New Deal he said in 1938 that "it will not be long before we have an American fascism"; in 1939 that its advocates had "no concern whatever for individual freedom . . . like Marx and Lenin and Mussolini"; and in 1940 that "There is a good deal more danger of the infiltration of totalitarian ideas from the New Deal circles in Washington than there will ever be from any activities of the communists or the Nazi bund."

It is difficult to say that this kind of nonsense is honorable; and in this he is not only "unique" and "typical of himself," but typical also of the voice of the conservative Republican as we have too often become used to it in the past few decades, in the phrases of Goldwater, which hardly need to be repeated, and in the intemperance of the *National Review*, for example, especially in its early years, before it succumbed, like the Buckleys, to middle age. When Taft said that "if Roosevelt is not a communist today, he is bound to become one," he was reaching exactly as Goldwater was later to prescribe to "extremism in the cause of freedom," but he was reaching also to the kind of lie that makes one join with Humphrey in his qualified salute to the man's honor.

He was not entirely honorable in his associations with, and efforts at dissociation from, Joe McCarthy: an issue on which one would have thought that a man of his boasted integrity, and with his passionate concern for individual freedom, would have recognized that there was only one honorable position for him to adopt. Neither was he entirely honorable in his attempts to reconcile his repeated exhortations against the communist menace in the world with his lifelong warnings against the dangers of intervention in its affairs; and in his criticisms of Truman's policy in Korea, in particular, he bewildered even his friends as he seemed to grasp at any stick with which to beat the administration.

What one is seeing in all this is more than just Taft, but the making of a conservative, in the circumstances of the Republican party's long exile from office. In the mold of his character may be found a pattern we can discover in his successors: a dogmatism which only those who are —and are likely to remain—strangers to office can afford; and at the same time an irascibility that often makes them combine their rigidity of principle with a carelessness about the means they employ.

Taft was not the out-and-out conservative in domestic

policy that legend has made of him. Of the contenders for the Republican nomination in 1920, he wrote that "It is necessary to nominate a moderate progressive who will defend the existing system but work out such constructive changes as will keep the Republican Party a party of constructive change." The positions he took in the Ohio Assembly between 1921 and 1926 show that he supported measures of urban relief; introduced a bill for the non-partisan election of judges; opposed the censorship of movies; favored a minimum wage bill for women; opposed a bill for the enforcement of prohibition; opposed the Ku Klux Klan; opposed a bill outlawing dancing on Sundays; and opposed the compulsory reading of Scripture every day in public schools. These were the positions of a "moderate progressive" who was particularly alert to any actual or threatened curtailment of civil liberties in social life.

Even after the introduction of the New Deal he was flexible in his attitude toward its social purposes. Already in his campaign for election to the Senate in 1938 he came "a little closer than before to accepting the New Deal"; and after the Second World War he moved openly and with deliberation to positions on public education and public housing that many conservatives refuse even today. In March 1946 he said that the "federal government has a secondary interest to see that there is a basic floor" from which everyone may enjoy the advantages of equality of opportunity; "the entire basis of American life is opportunity . . . no child can have an equal opportunity unless he has a basic minimum of education." It was characteristic of what Arthur Schlesinger, Jr., once called his "basic respect for fact" that after a congressional tour of Puerto Rico in 1943 he expressed his shock at the poverty he saw there and confessed that the Puerto Ricans were adopting a number of socialist measures, "some of which are necessary." This was not a man whose mind was closed to the evidence or the meaning of all that was happening around him.

Yet the impact of the New Deal did close a part of his mind; and the measure of that impact may be taken in the fact that the conservative mind in America is still closed in much the same way. It was the political rather than the social impact of the New Deal that most disturbed Taft and other conservatives. They began to see a leviathan growing in the federal government, and especially in the presidency; and it is doubtful if they would have been as alarmed if the Democrats had not, at election after election after election, been returned both to the White House and on Capitol Hill. In the extreme reactions of the conservatives to the New Deal, one feels that they began to think that some gigantic conspiracy was being worked against them. Arthur Vandenberg was "one of alliteration's most conspicuous and pitiable victims," an observer said at the time, and in a speech in 1940 he said that people were tired of "bureaucrats, boondoggles, barnacles, brains trusts, ballyhoo, and bankruptcy"; but in an asinine form he was giving expression to a conservative fear—which had some justification—that a federal structure was being created that was an arm of the Democratic party.

We must bear this in mind as we read Taft's denunciations of the encroachments of the federal government and the expansion of the presidency. There was much in his warnings that should have been heeded more at the time —not least by the liberal Republicans who then opposed him, and now try belatedly to occupy his positions—but the exaggerations and rancor that too often accompanied them were partly a result of an otherwise reasonable fear that the Democratic party was making of the federal government a vehicle for its partisan ambitions.

He was within the boundaries of reason when he questioned "the centralization of power that was placing the executive branch above Congress and the courts." He was right in saying that there is in the American system "no principle of subjection to the executive in foreign policy," and even, two weeks after the attack on Pearl Harbor, that "criticism in time of war is essential to the maintenance of any kind of democratic government." He was also right in saying that "A democratic government cannot prohibit strikes" and remain democratic. But he was not right in suggesting not merely that the New Deal was "socialism with a vengeance" but that it must (and already was) leading to a totalitarian regime, which he indiscriminately labeled either communist or fascist.

He also expressed a searching and traditionally conservative fear of modern war, and of its impulse to collectivism. He said in 1940 that war would mean "the terrible destruction of life and property, and the practical establishment of a dictatorship in this country through arbitrary powers granted to the President, and financial and economic collapse." A few months later he lamented that "we are certainly being dragged towards war and bankruptcy and socialism all at once"; and still later that "before we get through with that war the rights of private property in the United States will be to a large extent destroyed." But he was not right to say in St. Louis on May 20, 1940, when Europe was collapsing before the armies and air force of Hitler, that American entrance into the war would be "more likely to destroy American democracy than to destroy German dictatorship." A man capable of such a statement had a rage in him.

As one watches the rage grow in him, one is aware that a part of it, at least, may be traced to a feeling of impotence: to the failure of the Republican party to choose him (or any other conservative, for that matter) as its presidential candidate, and to its equal failure under those whom it did choose as its standard-bearers to win the White House. He became an extremely skilled and tenacious leader in Congress. Arthur Krock of the *New York Times* once said that he was a MacGregor: that wherever he sat, there was the head of the table. Another political journalist in 1947 found that "Congress now consists of the House, the Senate, and Bob Taft." After the inauguration of Eisenhower in 1953, Richard Rovere said that Taft had "ascended new heights of power and prestige" in the Senate, and that his power reached even to the House of Representatives, where he gave his attention to the "most obscure subcommittees." But in spite of all his resistance to the encroachments of the presidency, he knew that it was there that power lay. "No one can question the duty of the executive to propose a definite program," he said in 1939. "The policy-making power of the President has always been the most dynamic force in America." For the greater part of his political life, any grip on this dynamic force was denied to him and his party.

He would probably have been a very aggressive President. The historian Richard Hofstadter was almost certainly right in saying that if he had been nominated and elected in 1952, "his administration might have been almost as disappointing to the hard core of the extreme right as Eisenhower's"; and this would probably have been equally true if Goldwater had been elected in 1964. But this has been the condition of the conservative Republican since 1932—on the outside, looking in—and when he does have a conservative in the White House, in the person of Gerald Ford, he is indeed disappointed. He is disappointed that power cannot at a stroke defy the realities and complexities of the modern world. So he rages.

But he rages also for another reason. Not only can he not control the modern world to his satisfaction, he does not really care to know it as it in fact exists. His own dream of America, as he has been able to construct and maintain it in his own life, is not to be despised; but it insulates him from the reality of America, as it exists for others, and as it is all around him every day for him to see, if only he would look. This insulation was almost impenetrable in Taft, a kind of blindness.

He had every reason to be aware of the effects of the Depression. In his own city of Cincinnati, they were terrible. By the end of 1934, 140,000 people, more than one fifth of the population of Hamilton County, were on relief. Yet in 1931, before the introduction of the New Deal, which helped to provide this relief, he had opposed even state-sponsored unemployment insurance in words whose precision is almost icy: "My inclination is very much opposed to any system which provides for the payment of money to men for doing nothing. I have no reason to think that a further study will change my mind." A further study of what? Of statistics or of a theory of government—or of the misery that was around him?

We must be clear that the lack of compassion was not personal. Conservatives are usually as kind as others when they are brought face to face with suffering. As a young lawyer, Taft said of his legal-aid work: "It is a sort of charity that I can really take some interest in. In fact I seem to be engaged in free legal work most of the time, and it might as well be for the poor . . . I do feel rather sorry for the indigent criminal." That voice is rather engaging, compassionate and self-deprecatory, as the voice of Goldwater can often be. But when to be "rather sorry" for the poor who were not visible, for the masses of people who were thrown into hopelessness by the Depression, was not enough, this compassion also was inadequate.

Neither his upbringing, nor his social background, nor the circles in which he moved, nor the law practice in which he was engaged by the end of the 1920s, nor his increasing absorption in fiscal questions in the Ohio legislature, gave him any real knowledge or awareness of "the needs of thousands of Cincinnatians who lived outside the world inhabited by the corporate leaders, bankers, and judges who joined him at the Queen City Club or at gatherings sponsored by the University Club." He was a prudent investor and, says his biographer, "emerged from the Depression as prosperous as before . . . [It was for him] more than anything else a confusing and disturbing interlude that did more to confirm his ideas than to push him in new directions." As one has said, what is lacking here is not personal compassion, but a compassionate social and political imagination.

At its worst, the lack of that imagination can sustain the kind of insensitivity shown by Taft's father during the Pullman strike in 1894. After violence had exploded between federal troops and strikers in Chicago, William Howard Taft wrote: "The Chicago situation is not much improved. They have only killed six of the mob as yet. This is hardly enough to make an impression." The career of the son provided no example of an insensitivity equal to that.

And yet there was the same kind of flaw. Felix Frankfurter put his finger on it in a letter to Erwin Griswold on July 31, 1952: "A man may have a fine reasoning and yet have disastrous premises. That's true of Bob— plus a total want of what I call the poetic sensibilities, sensitiveness to the feelings and needs of other people. He is not the only high standard product of our [Harvard Law] school of first-rate reasoning capacity, but without insight into the nature of man and the great current of society." One might say the same of as personally decent a man as Goldwater: "a want of the poetic sensibilities, sensitiveness to the feelings and needs of other people," and this lack of imagination in turn produces an insularity that must lead to a kind of rage, if the cries of those who are in need and less advantaged than oneself seem to be only a clamor from ignorant or idle people of whose condition one personally knows very little.

The exaggerations that are a result of this rage are too similar in Taft and, a generation later, Goldwater, to be overlooked. The first could say that he feared the New Deal in Washington more than the Communists or the Nazis. Goldwater in 1959, in a debate with Stewart Udall on federal aid for schools, could say almost the same: "Yes, I fear Washington more than I fear Moscow." These are the remarks of men who do not feel at home in their own country in their own time, who do not trust its people because they do not know them, and do not trust its institutions because they have for so long not commanded them; and out of this feeling of impotence, so evident in Taft, the conservative in America in this century has been made.

The Mobile Home
of Conservatism

IF THE LIBERAL REPUBLICANS have been unable to make
a "home" for their party in the East—in the sense that
Fortune sighed in 1937 that the Democrats had always
had one from which to build in defeat—a similar criticism
can be made of their conservative critics. No less interested an advocate of a Southern Strategy than John Tower,
the senator from Texas, said in 1976 that Reagan, during
his campaign for the nomination, always seemed to think
that he could go on to win the election without carrying
for his party the six most populous states in the Union.
One sometimes has the feeling that the "home" from
which the conservatives hope to win an election is really a
mobile home, which moves from parts of the Midwest,
down through the Mountain States, across the desert to
California, and then—whoosh!—through the Sun Belt
to Florida. Whether in 1964 or today, it is hard not to
wonder if any conservative Republican has a map of the
electoral college in his head or his pocket.

One of the weaknesses of the conservative position is
that it rests on the belief that there are unnumbered—but
enough—conservative electors "out there" who are just
waiting to vote if they are given what Goldwater called

an "alternative." But this is untrue. Every election study and statistic emphasizes that it is the Republicans, and especially the conservatives, who are most likely to go to the polls. They are better educated, have more time, can get to the polling stations more easily, and are better organized; and anyhow it is a truth, not very difficult to appreciate, that those who have something to defend are more likely to vote than those who can only hope, with not much conviction that they will get it, for what they have not got.

It is precisely for this reason that the liberal Republicans have argued for so long that the party cannot expect to be returned to power unless it attracts the independents and a substantial number of disaffected Democrats. This was the basic appeal of Eisenhower; and in fact one of of his most important decisions after his nomination was to ignore the strategic plan of the Republican National Committee that was presented to him at the Brown Palace Hotel in Denver, in August 1952, and which argued that the efforts of Willkie in 1940 and of Dewey in 1944 and 1948 to woo the so-called dissenting or liberal but uncommitted vote had ended only in disaster. To the liberal Republicans, the strategy of the right wing in the past half century has seemed, as the Ripon Society put it in the 1960s, to be one only for "consolidating a minority position," an attempt to build "a coalition of all who are opposed to something."

At its nuttiest—no other word will do—this search for a new coalition led Richard Nixon, in a CBS radio broadcast on May 16, 1968, to say that a new political alignment had evolved that was composed of Republicans, liberals, black militants, and the "new South"; and that he was its leader!

But as the conservative Republican gets more accustomed to capturing or influencing the presidential nomination of his party, he becomes as ingenious, and seems at least as plausible, as the liberal Republican in proving that the Republican party now has a "home." He takes his slide rule to measure demographic shifts from one region to another; he computes the rise in income of groups and classes, and the spread of affluence and even of property; and from such elaborate calculations he, as well as the liberal, has produced his prognostications of an "emerging Republican majority." But somehow these never really translate into convincing evidence in the electoral college that the Republicans have replaced the Democrats as the normal majority party. They may win, but they do not win in such a way that they may then command. Their victories are still like forays into enemy territory.

For it must again be emphasized that one is not saying that the Republican party is unable ever to capture the White House—or, for that matter, Congress—but that it does not yet seem able to capture them in a way that gives the feeling that it is occupying the country. Even when it gains power, it still governs as if it were governing *against the country;* and in this Richard Nixon did not only reflect his own political character, but also his party's sense of its own weakness. The unhappy fact is that the Republicans have not yet found their way back into the heart and mind of their country, and so they diddle with their charts of where groups or classes of dissident voters may be found.

The "emerging Republican majority" has been supposed to find one of its "homes" in the South. But when the Republicans began to conceive a Southern Strategy in the 1950s, and to get excited about it in the 1960s, they were really devising one for the time of the Dixiecrat rebellion in 1948. They saw that the South was changing—otherwise how could they expect it to go Republican?—but not how it was changing. They seemed in 1976 to have no idea why one of Jimmy Carter's advisors was able to say of the South: "Jimmy has the blacks, hc has the farmers, he has the rednecks: who else is there?" Like all such illuminating political remarks, there was of course exaggeration in this. But one could hear the Republicans stutter: "Well, there are all those 'new' Southerners, in the 'new' middle class, in the 'new' industries, in the 'new' cities, in the 'new' suburbs, and *we* were going to join them to the rednecks and the Wallace constituency, and to everyone who is fed up with the Feds."

But after almost thirty years in which the Democratic party has been disrupted in the South, and although its hold on the South is looser than before, things have not happened that way. At the Republican Convention in 1976, Gerald Ford even let it be known that he was conceding the "Cotton South," reviving an old Republican term of abuse, and then wasted his time trying to win it.

The agitation of the white Democrats in the South was already obvious before Franklin Roosevelt died, and it became even more clear during the Fair Deal of Truman. In 1947, Harold Stassen told a meeting in Orlando, Florida: "I believe that the time has come for the development of a genuine two-party system in the South. . . . You can be—you *should* be—a Republican Party of the South." On November 26, 1951, Winthrop Aldrich—one of the Eastern Establishment leaders who was trying to persuade Eisenhower to run for the nomination—wrote to the general that Governor Allan Shivers, a Texas Democrat, had confided to him that Eisenhower's nomination would provide "a very good chance of bringing the Southern Democrats and the Northern Republicans together in some permanent manner." In the event, Eisenhower did quite well in the South in 1952, and he of course did very well in 1956, when even the blacks left the Democratic party in substantial numbers, largely on the issue of civil rights, as it was summed up in the slogan: "A vote for the Democrats is a vote for Eastland."

But the fundamental fact about the Eisenhower victories was that the South, especially in the cities, divided its votes much as did the rest of America. Leaving aside the exceptional circumstances of 1956, Eisenhower in 1952 did handsomely in the upper-income precincts; Adlai Stevenson did as well in the lower-income districts. A myth of the "changing South" was thus born on the basis of an economic stratification that must leave the Republicans in almost as much of a minority as before.

It was after 1956 that the Republican party formed a southern division under Lee Porter, who labored at his tasks with some success, but with no obviously significant breakthrough for the Republicans. Richard Rovere noticed very early the strategy they had chosen: "Winning back the Negroes [in the North] would mean forfeiting much of what the Republicans had gained in the South . . . . [Party managers] were more disposed toward strengthening their present alliance with conservative Southerners than toward reviving the old one with Northern Negroes." But as the great push for civil (including voting) rights began in the 1960s, under two Democratic administrations, it was not only the northern blacks the Republicans had forfeited, but the southern blacks as well, to gain temporarily an advantage with some southern whites.

This was one of the most profound errors ever committed by a great party; and we can be sure that a Theodore Roosevelt would not have made it in the circumstances. But what of the disaffected white Southerners? Could not the Republicans attract and hold them in sufficient numbers? "The alienation of the South from Lyndon Johnson and the national Democratic Party was complete by 1964," said Stewart Alsop in 1967. But that was not true, not even of 1964. "The Southern strategy presupposes, everyone knows," wrote the *National Review* in February 1964, "that Barry Goldwater shall be the Republican candidate." Goldwater was the candidate, and look what happened. He carried the five states of the Deep South (Eisenhower had carried four in 1956), but he failed to carry one other Southern state; and in the electoral college, he had only 47 out of 128 votes from the South. If one has victories like that, defeats are not necessary.

Obsessed with shifts of population, with the upper-income precincts in the "new cities," with the new industrialization and urbanization, the Republicans did not seem to know or understand the South. Insofar as it has ever been "solid," it did not become the solid South for the Democrats as a result of the Civil War; the Republicans were still holding substantial support in the eleven ex-Confederate states into the 1890s. It was only after the Populist upheaval at the end of the last century that the supremacy of the Democrats became complete, so that Theodore Roosevelt could say in 1901 that there was no longer a Republican party in the South, "simply a set of black and white scalawags."

Southern society, and therefore Southern politics, have always been much more complex than most northerners have understood. The South has always been "internally at odds with itself," as one observer has put it. "The conflicts that have been so much a part of the Southern experience have occurred . . . between Southerners and within Southerners, as much as between North and South"; and in this century that has meant between and within the Democrats, who, in surviving the civil rights struggle, with "the blacks, the farmers, the rednecks" still with them, are merely repeating their history. This was especially apparent in the failure of the Dixiecrat rebellion. "The most substantial political leaders in the region," says Dewey Grantham in his study, "shied away from the Dixiecrat radicals and were careful to keep lines of communication open with the national [Democratic] party leadership"; as of course George Wallace himself was always careful to do.

One ought not to be surprised at all this. In a long journey through the South in 1965, the year after the Goldwater campaign, and while the fury of the white South at the civil rights legislation of Lyndon Johnson was at its crest, it was possible to search out many of the "new" Republican leaders, and what was striking about them was that so many seemed not to be and in some cases were not—Southerners at all. They did not really have a feel for the significant divisions that had divided the states of the Southwest, such as Texas and Oklahoma, so quickly from the other Confederate states after the Civil War; or for the struggles between the eastern plains and the western hills on the Atlantic seaboard; or those between the delta and the piney woods in the Deep South; or for the complexity of the social divisions that the Democrats know like their knuckles; or for the "habit of radicalism" that Populism had not created but helped to ingrain.

No one who knew anything of all this, and understood its importance, could have imagined with Lee Porter, in the guidelines he issued for Republicans in the South, that all they had to do to establish themselves was to "capitalize fully on the rebellion against radicalism" which he thought the Dixiecrats represented. But even worse, anyone who believed, after the failure of the Dixiecrats, that a Southern Strategy could be put together without the blacks at the heart of it knew nothing of the South, the distribution of its population, its history and its lore, its rebellions and its heartbreaks, its voice and its music, its pity and its pride.

There is more justification for regarding the Southwest as a home of the Republicans. It certainly has all the characteristics of the mobile home in which the Republicans seem now to live. The South has roots; much of the Southwest has none, and rootlessness in his own country is today the character of the Republican.

But in terms of votes in the electoral college, the Southwest, even the new and expanding Southwest, looks a little skimpy, unless it can carry with it the southern states to its east, and California to its west. But not only are the Republicans still weak in the South, it is just as true that California has never been, is not now, and does not seem ever likely to be a stable home of the Republican party in terms of national politics. California is peculiar to itself; indefinable and chameleon. Once over the Sierra Nevada, the rest of the Southwest seems very remote. "Houston," one says in Los Angeles, and people ask: "Where? . . . Oh, you mean Houston . . . that town over near Louisiana."

Whoever invented the concept of the Sun Belt knew his journalists. Journalists are much more likely to be captured by a phrase than they are to invent a phrase with which to capture their readers. A phrase like Sun Belt is as birdlime to them: They alight on the twig and stick to it. No sooner does someone talk of a Sun Belt than they all discover (a) that there is a belt of states that stretches across the south of the United States, and (b) that the sun shines on it more than it does on the belt of states that is strung across the north of the United States. Q.E.D: There is a Sun Belt of political significance.

The trouble with too many political observers is that they fly into large cities, like Houston or Phoenix, and fly out twenty-four hours later usually having seen only the same people as other political observers. But the new big cities like Houston and Phoenix are deceptive. It is only a slight exaggeration to say that they are pasted on the map, and that a quick visit to them gives little idea of their hinterlands, and even less of the states to which they belong.

Houston is a comparatively old city that has become new. Its own social structure and its relationship to the state of Texas are difficult to understand and to disentangle. Anyone who has lived in Houston for any length of time begins to realize that it is whichever freeway off the Loop that one takes out of it. You may choose to go in any one of seven directions: in half an hour you will be in one of seven distinct regions of the state. To talk of carrying Texas in a presidential election is, of course, to talk of accumulating a statewide popular majority; but if one then talks of how to accumulate that majority, one has to look out from Houston or Dallas, from Corpus Christi or even Austin, to regions and counties in which are ingrained separate histories and folk memories that have only to be touched to become politically alive. Since the one-party politics of Texas was first seriously disturbed in the 1950s, forcing men as powerful as Sam Rayburn and Lyndon Johnson on to the defensive in their own state, there is no way Texas can be assumed to be a part of any Sun Belt; and without a state as large as Texas —as without a state as large as California—what does the concept of the Sun Belt mean? Perhaps Texas will in any given year go Republican (as in 1952 and 1956) or Democratic (as in 1960 and 1964); but all this says is that the Southwest is today no more reliable a political region than the Sun Belt of which it is supposed to be a part.

The more one tries to take seriously the concept of the Sun Belt, the more the impossibility of defining it in any significant political terms reminds one of an English verse.

> The rain it raineth every day
> Upon the just and unjust fella:
> But more upon the just because
> The unjust hath the just's umbrella.

The sun also does not fall equally and to the same effect on people in the same region, or even in the same state. The sun does not make California like Florida; any more than it makes California like its sunny neighbors, Nevada and Arizona, or Florida like its sunny neighbors, Georgia and Alabama. It does not even cause the same things to grow or happen in Florida as in Louisiana, in Texas as in California. It is not the only element in the climate, and the climate is not the only element in the environment. There is no Gulf Coast Highway, as there is the Pacific Coast Highway; and that just about says it all.

Even the industrialization of the South and the Southwest has not been of the same character, or had the same effect, in Georgia as in Arizona, in Texas as in California: booming Atlanta is not at all like booming Houston; Phoenix has little in common with San Diego; and nowhere else in the whole stretch of the Sun Belt are there two cities like San Francisco (if one can count it as a sun city) and Los Angeles. The agricultures of the two great states of Texas and California are marvelous; they are both miracles of husbandry, wonders of the world. But they are not alike, neither in their products, nor their methods, nor their marketing, nor their organization, nor their employment. The sun shines on them both, but in different ways, to produce different crops by different methods, and so to create different societies.

At the time of the Republican Governors Conference in 1966, David Franke, the former editor of *New Guard,* the official organ of the Young Americans for Freedom, a conservative organization, produced a report for the American Conservative Union. In it he said: "Republican governors, once the bastion of liberalism within the party, have undergone a dramatic shift toward conservatism," and he mentioned Kirk of Florida, Reagan of California, Babcock of Montana—three governors from three states with very little in common. To find the evidence of a firm conservative base in them was like seeing a circus elephant stand on three legs, and imagining that that is how it normally supports itself.

One is not denying—it was acknowledged earlier in this argument—that there is now, as there has for a long time been, a deep conservative inclination west of the Mississippi and south of the Mason-Dixon line; and it is fundamentally healthy to see both these states and the conservative inclination in them find their voice on the national scene, after the long domination of the North and Northeast. But that is very different from saying that something new, of immediate and unforeseen impact on politics, has begun to manifest itself in a particular region (or regions) of the country, which suddenly are displaying a novel and significant uniformity.

There is no evidence that such a uniformity exists where both the conservatives and the Republican party in general look for their home. Reagan fought for the nomination of his party from a base in California in which he had already been succeeded as governor by a Democrat. Florida was the state in 1976 in which Jimmy Carter chose to put an end, once and for all, to the right-wing movement of George Wallace, and did so. John Connally has only a shadow of the power in Texas that Tom Connally once possessed, as the 1976 election showed. One may put it in another way: It is unbelievable that the Republican party will ever establish the kind of hold on Texas that made Sam Rayburn and Lyndon Johnson simultaneously the Speaker of the House and Majority Leader of the Senate. *The very forces that have undermined the hold of the Democrats on the South and Southwest—and* nothing deserves more emphasis than this—*are the same forces that must preclude the Republicans from establishing a similar hold.*

Every theory of an "emerging Republican majority"—whether it is conceived by the liberals or the conservatives—rests on the belief that a coalition may be put together, that a home may be found, in the same way the Democrats once did it: by searching out the interests and groups, the classes and regions, that may be forged into a reliable union. But just as the Democratic party has found that times have changed, one would have thought that the Republican party would realize that the opportunities that have thus been presented to it are different from those on which the Democrats for so long built their power: that a coalition of regions and classes, groups and interests, is no longer the clue they should be following.

But follow it they do—to an important extent under the influence of an academic political science in America which is so tied to the methods of quantitative measurement that it does not know any other way of judging political behavior and motives—and so turn dizzily from a Southern Strategy in one decade to the promise of a Sun Belt in the next; and even fish around in the suburbs in the belief that there they have discovered some new species of humanity, the middle class come into its own.

What the Republicans, liberal or conservative, basically like about the South and Southwest (and of course the

West as well) is that they think that these basically are WASP, which is one reason they keep ignoring the importance of the fact that at the western stretch of the Sun Belt lies California, and at its eastern stretch lies Florida. Somehow the mass immigration of the end of the last and the beginning of this century still passes by the Republican, however much he may from time to time look expediently for support among the "ethnics." He is still convinced that somewhere the true American may still be found: English and respectable, Protestant and in business, and there he is, it is thought, in the suburbs of the Sun Belt.

Misinterpreting the Suburbs

PERHAPS MORE NONSENSE IS talked about the suburbs than about any other social or economic group in the United States. There is a widespread misconception among those who do not live in them that the suburbs are entirely populated by people who are at least reasonably affluent, who are sufficiently content with their lot not to be bothered very much to try to improve it or to associate their own discontents with those of others who are less fortunate, who are antiblack and spend all their days grousing about those who are on the welfare rolls, and who want only to be left alone, to enjoy their untrammeled lives of libertarian impulse, on their lawns and their patios, among the forsythia or the tulip trees or the oleander, according to where they live. In short, the dwellers in the suburbs are selfish and shortsighted, greedy and stupid: at least that too often is the picture that the Republicans paint of them.

Even the Democrats have been overwhelmed in recent years by the thought of these bovine families, grazing mutely off their crabgrass. Lawrence O'Brien, later to be the chairman of the Democratic National Committee, reminded a Western States Democratic Conference in

Los Angeles in 1967 of "American workers who live in the suburbs, pay taxes, support churches and community activities, and hope to send their children to college." After his defeat by Reagan in 1966, Pat Brown did not blame himself, he blamed the suburban dwellers: "Workers used to ask about workmen's compensation and disability insurance. Not this time. The workers have become aristocrats, and when they become aristocrats they become Republicans"; to which one can say only that they must have a peculiar conception in California of the attributes of both aristocrats and Republicans.

The attempt to turn the suburban dwellers into a uniform class—of uniform interests and uniform aspirations, usually with motives of only the narrowest self-concern— is insupportable as well as a demeaning of them. If one takes the Long Island Railroad (not something to be recommended to aristocrats) out to the Hamptons, at what point is one among these uniform aristocratic workers, at what point does one leave them behind? Where on the Philadelphia Main Line?

There are even black suburban communities. Not long ago, at a meeting of people drawn from suburban communities in Philadelphia, the only native-born Main Liner was a black woman. There are Jewish suburbs, long established and newly springing, that do not fit into the imagined mold; and there are other complex ethnic suburbs, where the ethnic heritage is not necessarily diluted by its transportation from the inner cities. It is at least as clear that many ethnics maintain their identities when they move to the suburbs as that any lose them. "Movement from the first settlement area may actually represent a transplanting of the ethnic community to suburbia," said one student in the *American Political Science Review* in 1967; and he also concluded that contacts with other groups do not necessarily weaken the self-awareness of the ethnic group. The suburbs are not a melting pot made fragrant with bouquets of antiperspirant.

No more are they of a single class, social or economic. In most suburbs, the majority do not have a college education, they do not work in managerial or professional positions, or own their own businesses, and they do not commute to jobs in the cities downtown. In the Chicago metropolitan area, how does one, for any significant purpose or to develop any political strategy that will work, put working-class Cicero into the same category as upper-middle-class Glencoe? Even the most middle of middle-class suburbs are not uniform. Even in them the kaleidoscope of American society still works: according to the angle from which one looks at it, the pattern changes and forms into a new pattern.

Of course there are some likenesses. During the Second World War, the Office of Facts and Figures, an agency of the government, put out a radio series called *This Is War*. In one of them, a boy was heard to say: "That's one of the things this war's about." A girl asked him: "About us?" And the boy answered: "About *all* young people like us. About love and gettin' hitched, and havin' a home and some kids, and breathin' fresh air out in the suburbs . . . about livin' an' workin' decent, like free people." It is easy to smirk at what seems to be the banality of this, to dismiss it as only crass and materialistic, and therefore as Republican, for it is the Republicans who now usually make this identification. But there is a kind of idealism in it, of wishing life to be better, of knowing that it can be made better, not only for oneself but for others; and that is not merely materialistic hope, to be appealed to at a merely materialistic level.

The basic assumption of the Republicans is that to move to the suburbs is to take another step to becoming WASP and middle-class. When the Republican strategist of the Eisenhower years, Robert Humphreys, tried to explain to Leonard Hall, the chairman of the Republican National Committee, some of the reasons for the severe defeat the Republicans suffered in 1958, he asked: "When you go to a Republican dinner, whom do you see at the head table? It is an even-money bet that the head table will be 100 percent white, Nordic, Protestant, upper-income class. Who gets introduced from the audience? Ditto above . . . a cross-section of the Republican Party is a mere splinter in breadth compared to a cross-section of America." If one were to conduct the experiment today, it would still be an even-money bet; and that is a tragedy for the party.

One might have expected, even hoped, that the conservative Republicans, with all their radical mission to revitalize American society, would cast their net wider.

But of those delegates and alternates from the Deep South to the Goldwater convention in 1964 who answered a questionnaire—a sufficient number to be a trustworthy sample—all were white; 75 percent were male; 74 percent had been to college; 74 percent were in managerial or professional occupations or were proprietors of their own businesses; 72 percent were in the upper-income groups; 75 percent said that they were Episcopalians or Methodists or Presbyterians (hardly a cross-section even of the Deep South); 31 percent identified themselves as upper middle class (compared with 19 percent of the adult population of the country), 67 percent as middle class (39 percent for the adult population), and only 2 percent as working class (56 percent for the adult population). These are alarming figures for any party that is seriously bent on governing.

In these figures about the Goldwater activists in the South, there is the intimation of all that is radically at fault both with the Southern Strategy—where are "the blacks, the farmers, the rednecks" among them?—and the "suburban strategy." Whether it is led by its conservatives or its liberals, the Republican party in its essential composition is still an enclave of the privileged, whose association with the less privileged majority of the country is slight, casual, unknowledgeable, intermittent, and in the end fake and often objectionable.

In 1966, the policy committee of the Republican party in the Senate issued a report that depicted the new "power group" in American politics as a professional, technical, and managerial, middle class: affluent, young, used to security in employment, well educated, and living or expecting to live in the suburbs. There is no way in which the great majority of the American people can be pictured in these terms. No party can hope to become the normal majority party of the country when its leaders and active members are so dissociated from the population, and compose a "power group" of a privileged elite.

In a report on *Changing Metropolitan Markets* in 1961, the Department of Commerce said that "It is a reasonable assumption that the 1960 Census is the last in which central cities will be more populous than the suburbs." Already by 1966 the suburban share of the metropolitan vote in the midterm elections was 56 percent. These are interesting facts, but what they do not mean is that a dispersal of the population from the central cities to the suburbs means also an abrupt change in political allegiance. In fact, it may well be true that the extensive movement to the suburbs in the past two decades has made them less, and not more, Republican than they were before. "1956 appears to be the last year in which suburbs were considered to be predominantly Republican," wrote a sociologist in *Social Forces* in 1969, and he went on to quote one survey in the mid sixties that found that of the suburbs examined one third were Democratic, and another study of blue-collar workers who had moved to the suburbs, which showed that they continued to vote Democratic. "Suburbs built in the 1950s," he said, "were moderately priced and populated with Democrats who continued to vote Democratic": a reminder of how important it is to get away from the notion, which may have been true until the 1940s, that the suburbs are places for the privileged, with the attitudes of the privileged.

Of 198 suburbs studied by another sociologist, it emerged that 20 percent of them had voted Democratic in 1948; 15 percent in 1952; 8 percent in 1956; 40 percent in 1960; and 75 percent in 1964: three quarters of them went to the Democrats in the Goldwater year, when the conservatives should have come tumbling out of their suburban homes to vote for an "alternative." In so far as these figures are to be trusted—which is always with a pinch of salt—they do suggest, what common sense by itself forces one to consider, that the more widespread the movement to the suburbs, in the past quarter of a century, the more the suburbs become not an enclave of the affluent but still the nation in its various aspects and divisions.

Before the election campaign of 1944, the finance committee of the Republican party in New Jersey sent out a letter appealing for funds. "Twelve years of the New Deal has leveled fortunes," it said; "therefore the former large contributors no longer write large checks. We must now look to thousands of contributors for sufficient financial support." It has to be said that the Republican party has not done all that badly from large contributors in the succeeding years; nevertheless the plea in the letter, all but thirty years old, does now sound as if it comes from another age. In the down-to-earth terms one would expect from a finance committee, here was a party acknowledging the narrowness of its base; and today it still querulously admits the same. It knows that it is a minority party; it wishes that it were not; but it never seems to inquire what in its beliefs, or in the interests it serves, keeps it that way.

In one of the earliest of his homilies to his Cabinet, on March 20, 1953, Eisenhower said to its members: "Now, we've all got to remember that we're called the business administration. In fact we invited that description, and it's fine—up to a point."

As we have said earlier in this argument, it is often hard not to wonder at some of the insights that fell from Eisenhower's mouth, and hard not to smile at them. After all, one of the marks of his administration, as Richard Rovere put it at the time, was that "Once Eisenhower has found a first-class automobile dealer, cotton broker, or razor manufacturer, to head a department, he has acted as if the public interest has been satisfied and his own responsibility discharged." Yet this questioning—even distrust—of businessmen in politics, of the interests they serve and the methods they think appropriate, was deep-seated in some of those who served Eisenhower best, and often rose irritably in him.

As his administration drew to an end in 1959, Robert Humphreys wrote for the chairman of the Republican National Committee what he called "Material for Off-Record Speech to Businessmen," a severe document in which he said that "if I had to choose between [businessmen and politicians] as to which had more integrity, I would lean towards the politicians." He added that "The belief of businessmen that 'politics needs business methods' is one of the great fallacies"; and the same was said by Emmet John Hughes, one of the closest of Eisenhower's advisors, when he noticed the moment in the administration when "the awful truth about business-like methods came, at last, to be suspected [by some members of Eisenhower's Cabinet]: politics might not be *like* business." What is more, it was not only these who distrusted the influence of business. With his usual individual outlook, even Taft wrote to Ben McGiveran on June 20, 1951: "I do not like to talk much about 'free enterprise.' That has too much the meaning that business-men shall be able to do as they please." And as Eisenhower constructed his first Cabinet, Taft wrote to another friend: "I don't like the fact that we have so many businessmen."

Almost twenty years before, Alf Landon had spoken of "the abysmal ignorance of the average businessman regarding politics." But two years later—and here we come to the crux of the difficulty for the Republicans— he declared: "The Chamber of Commerce is the Ameri-can spirit in action, expressed by deeds not words." In the end the bouquet is thrown to business, the supremacy of politics over business is denied, and the Republican party finds itself thrust back to its narrow base. The majority of Americans are not businessmen, and never will be businessmen, are not members of the chamber of commerce, and never will be members of it. A party fall-ing back on so narrow a base is bound to be a minority party.

The dilemma faced by the Republicans in the past has been "the dilemma faced by politicians," as Rovere once said, "who must get their campaign funds from the rich and do their campaigning among the not so rich." In fact, the Republican party has more to gain from a reform of campaign financing than anyone else: It might at last be released from the narrow base to which it has been con-fined. A great party cannot build its leadership or its support on Rotary Clubs, any more than it can on a hand-ful of Jaycees, or on the National Association of Manu-facturers, or on corporation lawyers. Business cannot be an overriding concern of a political party, without its ab-dicating a part of its function.

Republicans in general, conservative or liberal, do not allow politics the preeminence which presumably a party exists to give it. Far more than actual differences in policy, although these matter, this is the essential difference between the two major parties in their attitude to the economy and therefore to the business world. Instinctively the Democrats acknowledge the preeminence of politics over other forms of social action, over other realms, whereas the Republicans do not; and it is hard to know not only how a party which denies this preeminence can govern well in the long run but why it should wish to govern, and so why it should have any real political instinct as a party wishing to gain power.

Ezra Benson, as Secretary of Agriculture in Eisenhower's Cabinet, gave so diminished a role to political action that he resisted the pleas to relieve the farmers' distress during a drought in the Southwest with the sublime plea: "We're doing all we can—we just need rain." His general policy was so negative that even other members of the Cabinet, such as Douglas McKay at Interior and Sinclair Weeks at Commerce, confessed that they "saw little virtue in taking conservative principles so literally as to assure in any national election the loss of fifty or sixty Midwestern electoral votes." When the Republicans in Congress voted to slash the appropriations for the Office of Education in HEW, Eisenhower erupted into another of his searing comments: "If any of those darn fools were running for reelection right now, they'd lose the vote of every liberal in the country, and that includes me." And again one must recall that on such questions as public housing and public education even Taft was impelled to move to a position far different from that of today's conservatives.

A party cannot hope to be great unless it intends to govern, as there could never be any doubt that Theodore Roosevelt always intended to govern. This is why the cry against "Washington" is a false cry for a party or a politician to raise. Even if only because he was a politician, Roosevelt could never have reached to the heresy that that government is best that governs least; and what is more, when it comes to the pinch, Republicans and conservatives do not reach to it either. On one occasion in 1939 Taft made the unqualified announcement in Des Moines, Iowa, that he opposed altogether the corn-loan policy of the New Deal. But on that very day the Department of Agriculture issued a 57 percent-per-bushel loan that poured as much as $70 million into Iowa, and the farmers of Iowa, Republican and even conservative, did not reject it.

There is something dishonest in the hollering of the Republican party at the activity of the federal government; but even from its own point of view it is misled by its own speciousness. Only a party with as narrow a base as we have just described, which expects to discover its leadership in a "power group" drawn from a new and affluent elite, could be convinced that the country is profoundly—not just reasonably—at odds with the federal government. Of the delegates and alternates questioned at the Goldwater convention, 94 percent thought that the government did too much; 95 percent disagreed that the federal government should find jobs for those without work; 93 percent disagreed that the federal government should help people to get medical care at low cost; 89 percent thought that all education should be left to state and local governments. These proportions bear no resemblance to those for the adult American population as a whole. They are the attitudes of a privileged minority who are strongly Republican party by their own heedlessness of the cares of others.

The Republicans who were taught by Theodore Roosevelt were agreed that "no amount of commercial prosperity . . . can in itself solve the terrible social problems which all the world is now facing." Even if one concedes that the prosperity in the United States is now greater and its benefits more widespread than then, even if one admits that the terrible social problems are today at least not so stark or so visible, the fact remains that prosperity is never by itself enough to satisfy a vigorous and an enlightened people. In the end, it palls; people grow restless if it is their only measure; they look for other values than those fed to them as satiated consumers; and it is one of the functions of politics to be alert to what it is that ails the spirits of men, not because it can provide the cure, that is to promise more than it can deliver, but because it can help to create the climate in which men will confidently join together to find their own cure.

Politics is not only the art of the possible, as is so blandly said by those who would like to persuade us that very little is possible; and certainly it is not the art of the impossible, as the utopians and the ideologues would like to have us believe. But it can and ought to be the art of the necessary, and there are necessary things for our societies always to do, of which politics must be one of the inspirers, beyond the creation and tolerably fair distribution of more prosperity. Among other things, it is necessary for men's health and fulfillment that they should feel that they are moral beings, moral members of a moral society; and although politics is not fitted to supply that moral sense, it must help to create the atmosphere in which it may develop and be fruitful, it must be one of the crystallizers and transmitters of it. When people cry out that their society is morally unsatisfying, politics cannot turn aside and merely ask the economy to provide more prosperity.

Ever since the New Deal, the Republican party has relied much too much on prosperity to return it to office or to keep it there. "The lesson the Republican Party should learn," wrote the editors of *Fortune* after the Republicans were devastated in 1936, "is the lesson that prosperity is still the best election argument." The truth in this is enough to be seductive; certainly a lack of prosperity, if one's own party has created it, is not a good election argument. But the truth is in the end slender, and enough politicians and parties in enough countries have had cause to grumble at the ingratitude of the people to remind us that prosperity is not ultimately or for long an argument on which a great party can rest.

What the conservative Republican, especially, has forgotten is precisely what in his dubious philosophizing he would claim to have most to teach his party: that people can and are moved by attitudes and persuasions, memories and hopes, which sometimes contradict their perceived economic interests, and certainly may cut across them. The conservatives in America are always in danger of reducing the voter to the very self-interested "economic man" whom they take the posture of detesting. Every one of their electoral strategies, for all the moralizing in which they are phrased, is fashioned on little more than the accumulation of group interests, which they believe to be dissatisfied; and they can never understand why the people who share these interests, like those in the suburbs, want the satisfaction of something more; the yearning to feel that the society to which they belong is good and compassionate, decent and generous, lofty in its ideals and exuberant in its pursuit of them; and that when they see in it from day to day a reflection of themselves, they do not wish to turn away and feel that they are less than they thought themselves to be.

The conservatives talk much of morality, and of the

immoralization of society in the modern age. But if one examines their moral vocabulary, one finds that it is a series of "thou shalt nots," directed only or primarily at one's own relationship with oneself—thou shalt not take drugs, thou shalt not be a homosexual, thou shalt not read pornography—which have fundamentally little bearing on how one behaves to others. But morality exists only in one's relationships with others, in the quality of one's attention to them; and in so far as politics must be alert to the moral disquiets of individuals and of the society of which they are members, it must be said that the conservatives and the Republican party they now so forcibly influence have abdicated one of the functions by which people can know that they are politically responsible.

A Long Grouse Against the Modern Age

No MORE ASTONISHING POLITICAL error has ever been committed in the past half century by the Republican party than the throwing away of the black vote, not only in the South but in the North, where historically it should have been the Republicans who were there to welcome the blacks as they began to arrive in the course of their own internal migration. Even on the ground of political expedience, few errors are more inexplicable; on any other ground, it suggests a lack of political sensibility that leaves one wondering whether the Republican party lacks not only political instinct but political imagination, whether they can imagine how opportunities can be made.

In the 1928 election, the Democrats began to weaken the traditional Republicanism of the blacks, partly as a result of the virulent attack which some southern whites made on Al Smith. With the split within the Southern Democrats, the blacks had again become a crucial factor in elections, and they were by no means then lost to the Republicans. Men such as Robert Moton, the successor of Booker T. Washington as president of the Tuskegee Institute, worked for Herbert Hoover in 1928; many influential black newspapers remained staunchly Republican.

And they had their reward: Hoover made no mention of the blacks in his inaugural address.

In 1932 there were important defections among blacks to the Democratic party. Robert L. Vann, publisher and editor of the *Pittsburgh Courier,* then one of the largest and most influential black publications in the country, repudiated Hoover and came out for Franklin Roosevelt. In a sentence that should have sent shivers down the spine of any Republican, he said: "My friends, go turn Lincoln's picture to the wall. That debt has been paid in full." In some of the northern cities, the bosses delivered the black vote to the Democrats, and depressed blacks voted for them in Pittsburgh and Detroit. But in other cities, the blacks still clung to the Republicans. Smith had polled thirty percent in the black wards of Cleveland; Roosevelt in 1932 polled only twenty-four percent.

The Republicans had still no reason to despair of the black vote. But when Franklin Roosevelt and Jim Farley went after such obviously valuable votes, the Republicans only slowly showed any sign of realizing what was happening to their situation. "The Negro vote is notoriously venal," wrote Dorothy Thompson in the *New York Herald Tribune* in August 1936, the voice of urban Eastern Republicanism speaking with civility. "Ignorant and illiterate, the vast mass of Negroes are like the lower strata of early industrial immigrants and like them are 'bossed' and 'delivered' in blocs by venal leaders, white and black." But even as she wrote, the black voters were beginning to respond to a policy, to the glimmerings of a new attitude to them in Washington. They migrated out of the Republican party in 1936 in droves, to vote for a program in which they found hope. Roosevelt's percentage of the black vote in Cleveland, for example, shot up to 62 percent; in Chicago it was 49 percent. The writing on the wall could not have been plainer.

The Republicans chose to ignore it in 1940, when the Democratic party for the first time included a frank appeal to the blacks in its party platform. By 1944, the blacks still remained loyal to Roosevelt, and the first twitch of rebellion in the white South could be felt. But it was exactly in 1944 that the Republicans should really have noticed what was taking place, as much in the North as in the South. In an analysis of the results, Herbert Brownwell, Jr., the chairman of the Republican National Committee, claimed that a shift of 303,414 votes in fifteen states outside the South would have given Dewey an eight-vote electoral college majority. But in at least eight of those fifteen northern states, the black vote exceeded the number of extra votes needed to move the states into the Republican column. Blacks were beginning to hold a balance in the North as well as the South.

What has happened since then is well enough known: the sticking by the Republican party to its decision to abandon the black vote in the North and South, in order to go after the white Democratic vote in the South, in pursuit of its Southern Strategy. Even when the 1956 election showed the ability of Eisenhower to attract the black vote, his administration and the Republican party itself did nothing in the four succeeding years to consolidate the gain.

The result has been that whereas the black vote between 1952 and 1960 constituted only 5 to 7 percent of the total Democratic vote, it rose to 12 percent in 1964, to 19 percent in 1968, and to 22 percent in 1972, even though in the same period the black population has remained a fairly steady 11 percent of the total population. Moreover, these black votes are strategically placed in the North in states with a large number of votes in the electoral college, a fact of which the Republican party was again reminded in 1976. In exchange, the Republican party has left itself to try to pick up the disaffected white vote in the South, in states with relatively few electoral votes, except for Texas. And what in 1976 was the reward for this folly: to see a white southerner carry the South and essential states in the North with the help of the black vote.

Something must be wrong with a party that even in terms of its own vitality and survival, can commit so disastrous an error; can turn away not only a strategic body of votes but a section of the population whose vitality is part of the life of the country. To forfeit the black vote, with no compensating advantage from the white vote, not reliably even in the South, not certainly even in the suburbs, needs an explanation beyond ordinary calculations.

Something is amiss. There is again something the Republican party does not seem to know or understand, or care to know and understand, in its own country in its own time. It is again as if it does not belong to the country, as if it feels that the country itself has passed it by; and it is left to pick up only the relics its rival has deserted, gathering the husks from which the grain has already been picked, an army only of the casualties, of dead leaves shaken from the tree where the new life is already preparing.

It is here that such of what has already been suggested may be drawn to a particular point. No one can seriously question that the entrance of the black in America into the heritage of his own country has been one of the great achievements of this century, something that America had to do, and which only America could do; and not to have wished or sought to be a part of this achievement, whatever the doubts, whatever the anguish, whatever the heartbreaks, not to have wanted to help to lead it and to give it direction, tells indeed of a lack of those "poetic sensibilities" for which Felix Frankfurter looked, and rightly looked, in a political leader and his party.

Do we not find here, as in so much else, a party that does not enjoy the century in which it lives, and must act? Gusto for the times in which we live: that is what one expects of a politician, and of a party that is engaged in politics. But the Republicans seem to distrust, dislike, and fear their own time. Almost the whole of twentieth-century conservatism had been one long grouse against the modern age; at best to disdain it. It is of course a tumultuous age, but one in which one may be enthralled and even elevated, certainly excited, simply by being alive in it. Some of the greatest ideas with which man has questioned his universe, his own place in it, and his own nature, have been working themselves out in our own lives, from Darwin to Marx, from Freud to Einstein. Yet all we get from twentieth-century conservatism—especially as it is represented in a work like Russell Kirk's *The Conservative Mind*, which was supposed to herald a rebirth of conservatism in America—is T. S. Eliot's plaint against the modern age: "We are the hollow men." The truth is that we are not. To have survived this century at all could hardly have been managed by men stuffed with straw.

The sour political voice of William Faulkner in particular runs through the conservative spirit in America in this century. One can hear the whole false prophecy in this Faulkner groan: "We—Mississippi—sold our state's rights back to the federal government when we accepted the first cotton price-support subsidy. . . . Our economy is not agricultural any longer. Our economy is the federal government. We no longer farm in Mississippi cotton fields. We farm now in Washington corridors and Congressional committee rooms." Every false note is there, every refusal to understand the way the world is turning, every acrid resistance to the twentieth century.

The disdain for the century all too easily translates into a disdain for the country in this century, as it now is. The party and the political movement—conservatism—that are supposed to be the most patriotic, and often accuse their opponents of being unpatriotic, in fact seem sometimes to detest the country as it has grown to be, and exists in the time that is here. Everything is wrong about it; it is going to the dogs. It would be hard to tell from some of their utterances what the conservative in America really likes about this country at the moment, except that it allows a few people to make a lot of money. The picture that he often gives in his protests is of a nation in which children no longer pray at school, adolescents are high on drugs, women abort their children, men and women want to be homosexuals, and the Constitution needs amending to stop the steepness of the decline.

The conservative is the last person on the Fourth of July in 1976 who could say, "Come home, America," because he himself does not really much like it here. He is as much an expatriate as conservatives like Eliot or Santayana; and if he is an internal émigré within the Republican party, at times the Republican party gives the impression of being an internal émigré in its own country.

No great political party—especially the party of Lincoln, one would have thought—sure of its own place, could have failed to be moved by the fact that at least the blacks, in our own century, were to become the Americans they are. It was an American fulfillment to be seized out of what a foreigner called an American dilemma: to be seized and wrought. Even if by nothing more, the very political instinct of a living party would have told where it should take its stance. The Democrats made their decision at their convention in 1948, but at no convention of the Republican party for forty years has the issue ever been seriously raised or debated or resolved.

The great English political journalist of the nineteenth century Walter Bagehot once wrote magnificently of the Cavalier (the predecessor of the Tory in England), and of his love of life; and at the end of the passage, he addressed the modern conservative, and said to him that if he wished to spread conservatism in society he should "try a little enjoyment." He should speak enjoyingly of his society and its thousand ways, its customs and its institutions; and he should be seen as a politician to enjoy the activity in which he is engaged.

One may say that the *National Review,* when it engages in the day-to-day polemics of politics, tries a little enjoyment. It is not as lusty as it once was—the responsibilities of advertising some of the lesser glories of the English language seem to have weighed on William F. Buckley, Jr.—but it still enjoys a good fight, and sometimes even a dirty one. But when one turns to its philosophizing, one finds that one is insinuated into a world of dread alarms, and of fear and distrust of all that now is.

At the Republican National Convention in 1940, Bruce Bliven very early observed what was going wrong: "In a dozen ways, the delegates to this convention showed that their dominating emotion was hatred—hatred of Roosevelt, hatred of the New Deal, hatred, it almost seemed, of the twentieth century." The fact that this observation was made by a liberal observer does not invalidate it. He was speaking of a hatred that sprang from fear, a hatred that was more than partisan, a hatred of the very time in which the delegates lived and must act.

This hatred of the twentieth century, growing out of the feeling that they did not belong to it anymore, that it had been preempted by enemies, reflected the fear which ever since has been an ingredient of conservative and so of some Republican attitudes. In 1956, Willmore Kendall —put forward by the conservatives as rather more profound a political philosopher than in fact he was—described himself in the *National Review* as one of those "who believes the United States—and the world—are on the edge of catastrophe." His language was always despairing: ". . . when the Communist glacier finally overtakes . . ."

was characteristic of his dirges. But if one believes in a free society and in free government, one had better trust in the warmth of its own free people, and in the ability of that warmth in time to melt any glacier; one had better believe that in time, knowing their institutions, they will know also how to use them.

This fear of the century, and of the country in which they live, accounts in large part for the willingness of both the Republican party as a whole and of the conservative movement in particular to sustain for so long, and certainly not energetically to oppose, the campaign of Joe McCarthy. The accusatory spirit is only another reflection of the fear and hatred felt at a world that is felt as unknown, and therefore seems menacing, and in which menace can be met only with menace. The casual attitude of many Republicans and conservatives to civil liberties grows out of a wish for a world in which known authority can make it seem safer.

The true conservative, with the politics of his country in his blood, delights in its skirmishes and battles, delights in difference, delights in his opponents; and he could never call his opponent a traitor. But this is exactly what the conservatives and the Republicans in America are too often found to be doing: finding traitors among those of their countrymen who happen to be their political opponents. The "enemies list" of the Nixon administration was not a peculiarity of his own licentious distrust of all humanity. It came out of a party: out of its distrust of its country, of its system of government, of its people, of its opponents, and perhaps above all out of a distrust of itself. They behave like aliens in their own country because that is how they feel.

The Republicans never seem to have had any awareness of the blacks as enjoying Americans who wanted only to be "let into" a country which, with all its faults, they still found good enough to wish to enjoy themselves in. It is as if they had never heard the sound of a black song, or seen the rhythm of a black dance, or watched the grace of a black athlete, or listened to the shout of a black congregation, all of them American, three hundred years and more in America, their culture part of its culture, its culture part of theirs. Most people and both parties had to get over the hump of color; but once over it, what is there to fear? To search for the answer to this question is to face the fact that the sickness of the Republican party may be even deeper than has been thought: that it suffers from an infection of the spirit that is fear itself.

Patriots Outside
Their Society

LET US TRY, THEN, to picture the Republicans as they have become in this century, for it is indeed remarkable that, in a nation which boasts of so extensive a middle class, this preeminently middle-class party finds itself so often in a minority, unable for half a century to establish itself nationally as a governing party. The decline cannot all be blamed on bad luck or poor leadership, or even on demographic changes or economic conditions. Parties are like beasts, we have said, known to foe and friend, exciting fear and allegiance. Their will to live, not unlike that of the elephant, is something to be found in themselves, until at last it subsides and they take themselves off to the secret graveyard. The lure of the graveyard has been strong in the Republican party in the past fifty years, and we have to look for the explanation in the characters of those who compose it.

We will call them John and Margaret, these Republicans whom we are trying to describe. There is a strong patriotic instinct in them. Their country can depend on them whenever it is threatened from without, and it can rely on them also to carry on, from year to year, much of the unsung workaday activity by which a society keeps going.

As much as any other Americans, and in many cases more so, they are joiners. They are the Elks, the Rotarians, the Lions, the Masons, and they are also the Chambers of Commerce and the Junior Chambers of Commerce. Much of the voluntary work of American society is done by John and Margaret. Yet when all this is said, it is at last difficult, even at the level of patriotism, to know to what their loyalty is given. This is why they appear too often to be loyal only to the Flag, without it seeming to carry much meaning for them beyond itself; even when they take the Oath of Allegiance, the fervor is genuine, but it is also suspect, too determined an affirmation, and one wonders what lies beyond it.

In his *The Philosophy of Loyalty,* a book which Republicans might read with reward, the American philosopher Josiah Royce says that "loyalty is not sufficiently emphasized. Our popular literature too often ignores it or misrepresents it. . . . The second danger lies in the fact that we all think too often of loyalty as a warlike and intolerant virtue, and not as the spirit of universal peace." These words might have been addressed to John and Margaret, who are indeed among the "true-hearted obscure people," and often undertake the work of loyalty in their own communities; but who also seem not to take it seriously enough in the end, unable to give it a deeper meaning for themselves and in the wider society, and so they seize all too quickly the occasions to make it "warlike and intolerant."

John and Margaret today are patriots outside their society, and we have already noticed some of the reasons. Fundamentally, they do not like the country in this century, and do not feel that they belong to it; they are committed to the defense of free enterprise, and yet find that modern capitalism, in its search for profit, consistently erodes the traditional values which they hold dear; they are deeply suspicious of the East and its Establishment, even though they may live there and it generates much of the wealth of the nation; they adhere to a nostalgic and almost primitive conception of the exceptionalism of America, and have a deep suspicion of Europe and its infections. When they are out among the woods and mountains, rivers and lakes of America—John is likely to be a hunter—they feel that this is still God's Own Country, untouched and even virginal: where sky and earth still meet as once they did on the whole continent, and man and his God are not at war.

There is idealism in all this; and it is not to be denied. But it is an idealism that is at odds with the rest of American society as it has grown and developed, and as it now is. John and Margaret are therefore consistently at odds with themselves. They are at once the most patriotic but deeply alienated of Americans, and this is the frustration of many Republicans, suspicious of what their society has become, and yet endlessly loyal to the country in which that society has grown.

Walter Lippmann touched on one aspect of this fifty years ago in his essay on Sinclair Lewis: "The America of Mr. Lewis is dominated by the prosperous descendants of the Puritan pioneers. He has fixed them at a moment when they have lost the civilized traditions of their ancestors brought from Europe, and are groping to find new ways of life. Carol [in *Main Street*] is the daughter of a New Englander who went West taking with him an English culture. In Carol that culture is little more than a dim memory of a more fastidious society; it merely confuses her when she tries to live by it in Gopher Prairie. Babbitt is the descendant of a pioneer; he is completely stripped of all association with an ordered and civilized life." At the beginning of the essay, Lippmann said that Lewis had struck this vein with the inauguration of Warren Harding, and had continued to mine it successfully under Calvin Coolidge—in other words, in the last years of real Republican dominance—and what must interest and even astonish us is that, when we encounter John and Margaret today, we are meeting much the same people with recognizably the same attitudes.

Beyond their own communities and their daily activities, to what can John and Margaret be loyal, which in their own eyes deserves their allegiance, and which would unite them to the wider society? Their churches are persistently abandoning the traditional forms and beliefs that they cherish; neither the high culture nor the popular culture tells them what they wish to hear, or what even reflects themselves and their fears and aspirations as they understand them; they defend the economic system in the name of private enterprise, and yet know that it is intricately regulated to the benefit of the large corporations; they wish values to be stable even though no other Americans are more mobile than they. Their loyalty and patriotism are at a loose end, ready to be stimulated at any time by a Taft with his evocation of the horse and buggy age, by a Goldwater with his promise to cleanse America, or by a Reagan with his clamorous opposition to "giving up" the Panama Canal: something else of what was once familiar and reliable to be given up, in a world that is already too uncertain and so threatening.

When John and Margaret respond to Ronald Reagan on the question of the Panama Canal, they do not think in terms of strategy, or calculate the threats to the security and prosperity of the United States. It is not really even the objection to America being "pushed around" that troubles them. Something familiar is being taken away: that is what is unbearable. It is being taken out of their atlases as they have known them since their schooldays, and their feelings are strong because so much else has been and is being taken out of their other maps of the social and personal values in which they were raised.

But John and Margaret are in an even deeper quandary, and we may turn again to another essay that Walter Lippmann wrote fifty years ago. He described the prosperity that the American people were enjoying during the Coolidge years—"As a nation we have never spent so much money on luxury and pleasure as we are spending now. There has never in all history been such a widespread pursuit of expensive pleasure by a whole people"—and yet these same people had installed in the White House a "frugal little man" who in his personal habits was the very antithesis of this flamboyant hedonism. They had not only installed him, but praised him extravagantly for being a Puritan, while they went on enjoying the opposite of a Puritan way of life. "Thus we have attained a Puritanism *de luxe* in which it is possible to praise the classical virtues while continuing to enjoy all the modern conveniences." Half a century later in our still more affluent societies, do we not still find in John and Margaret, in the Republican party and especially in the conservative movement within it, the same ambivalence, the same

Puritanism *de luxe,* the same unconvincing and unsatisfying effort to escape?

Like their parents and grandparents, John and Margaret today put much of their energy into general social issues, rather than into the more genuinely political questions. Prohibition, the Klan, fundamentalism, Romanism, immigration: these issues of half a century ago have their counterparts today in drugs, the Equal Rights Amendment, abortion, homosexuality, pornography, and still immigration. Lippmann said that the earlier issues were simply "an extreme but authentic expression of the politics, the social outlook, and the religion of the older American village civilization making its last stand against what looks to it like an alien invasion. . . . The evil which the old-fashioned preachers ascribe to the Pope, to Babylon, to atheists, to the devil, is simply the new urban civilization, with its irresistible economic and mass power." Half a century later, John and Margaret are still offering the same resistance, trying to stem the tide of the "metropolitican spirit" of the large cities, and yet their resistance is again *de luxe.* From the ground of affluence, they try to oppose its hedonism it creates.

Nothing is more misleading than to talk of them, as a writer in *Fortune* did in 1977 and others have done, as forming a "neo-populist reaction." If they were populists at all, they would be populists *de luxe,* a label that makes no sense. They enjoy more than a mean share of the nation's wealth, and this is a part of their frustration. They stand outside their society, perhaps more than they realize, disliking the way it is going, but that society does well by them. It hardly honors them, and may even not pay much serious attention to them, but it pampers them. It may not give them leadership, but it gives them goods. It supplies them with golf courses and tennis courts, boutiques and discos, supermarkets and gourmet shops, and John and Margaret take them all.

You take your leisure, say the elites, and leave the running of society to us. But John and Margaret are activists; as we have said, they are joiners; they want to participate, to make a difference. So they are left to respond to the appeals or the manipulation, whichever way one looks at it, of a Goldwater or a Reagan who offers them the opportunity to act. Following the banners of such men, they feel that they can at least still participate, vote with their feet from their automobiles, that they are influencing the course of events; and it is a tragedy that the established leaders of the Republican party, over so many years, should have failed to excite these "true-hearted obscure people" to work more effectively within its organization.

John and Margaret lack leadership, not only within their own party, but from what, for lack of another term, we call the elites in American society, and in part they lack it because they reject it, the Establishment they despise. We have seen how *Fortune* pondered melancholically on the defeat of the Republican party in 1936; and in 1977 it was almost rewriting the same article under the headline, "The Unmaking of the Republican Party." Its author noticed that "before and during the New Deal years, it was the case that the Republicans were the Establishment Party. Today all this has changed." He said that with the rising tide of affluence, advancing technology, and the growing importance of knowledge and communication, higher education has produced an intelligentsia of unprecedented numbers and influence. Whether in colleges or universities, or in local, state, and national government, this intelligentsia forms a "higher-education establishment," which one would hardly expect to support the Republicans, the party more strongly inclined to resist educational expenditures. This is what Irving Kristol calls the "new class," a term as seductive as it is rhetorical and misleading.

According to Kristol, an intellectual who had made himself the mouthpiece of the non-intellectual, this new class of a vastly expanded and, he would say, half-baked intelligentsia stands against the business elites of sound sense and a practical cast of mind, the kind of men who meet a payroll. But as the *Fortune* article notes, we are today seeing "acted out the final chapter of the fall of the Republican Party from Establishment status—the falling away of big-business leadership. The fact that the G.O.P. is on the verge of seeing its special relationship with corporate business come to an end is a telling indication of how much the party has ceased to be an instrument of elites." This is all true, as far as it goes, but it does not go far enough back. For as we have seen earlier, a significant

122

proportion of the rank and file of the Republican party began to distance itself from the Eastern and business Establishment leadership of the party even in the 1930s.

Fortune notes an acute hostility to big business among the rank and file—as if it was not already incipient forty years ago—and there is of course no reason why John and Margaret should feel in any way attached or grateful to the corporate elite. For one thing, there is not all that much difference between the corporation executives and the new class, a fact which Kristol does not take into account, although it undermines his thesis. The business executives are also products of the vast expansion in higher education, of the demands made by an advancing technology, of the need for knowledge and communication; and between a junior executive of Mobil Oil and a staff aide on a Congressional committee that is concerned with the energy problem, the differences are barely discernible in background or education, temper or attitude or ambition. The traffic of talent that takes place between the universities, government and big business is the traffic of people all of whom belong to the new class. On the whole, they do not share the attitudes of John and Margaret to the social issues that trouble them, so that John and Margaret are left to find such leadership as they may in the scattered residues of an older and defeated system.

When it announced its beliefs in its first issue, the *National Review* said that "the largest cultural menace in America is the conformity of the intellectual cliques," and that "the most alarming single danger to the American political system [is] an identifiable team of Fabian operators . . . bent on controlling both our major parties." But since these "intellectual cliques" and "Fabian operators" are to be found in the large corporations as well as in the universities, in government and of course in the media, and since they are "bent on controlling" all the major institutions of the country and not only the two major parties, John and Margaret receive very little leadership from, and themselves have very little influence on, that section of society that creates not only the wealth of the country but its mind and culture and mores. Their future is being made without them, hence their sad condition as patriots outside their society.

For almost fifty years, neither the liberal nor conservative leaders in the Republican party have made any serious attempt to accustom John and Margaret to contemporary society, so that they may indeed act effectively in and on it, their voice with its necessary corrections of the way in which things are going at last to have an influence, and not merely be a defiant challenge to the tide to flow back. The liberals have despised John and Margaret, until at last they have taken their revenge. The conservatives have merely confirmed John and Margaret in the most senseless of their prejudices, with a cynicism that is not often noticed but is hard to forgive. There is something in Goldwater and Reagan and in the *National Review* that plays too facilely with the troubled cares of John and Margaret, which invites them as allies in the cheapest way possible, by telling them what they want to hear without ever quite taking it seriously.

The failure of the Republican party to become a genuine and acceptable conservative party in the twentieth century is the failure of its leaders, liberal and conservative, to encourage and compel John and Margaret to establish a rapport with other groups in their society who are unlike them; and this is partly because they have failed to encourage or compel them to establish such a rapport with other groups within their own party. To the inclusiveness of the Democratic party we will come; it may well be too inclusive. But the exclusiveness of the Republican party, its failure to offer a home to the immigrant in the first half of this century and to the black as an internal immigrant in the second half, is a sentence of death on any political party in any country that practices democracy. You cannot keep significant groups of people out of your party and still hope to know it.

From this comes the fear: the fear of a society that is unknown, so that one stands outside it as unknown, like John and Margaret, with their true-hearted patriotism running to waste, and at times even to a mean-spiritedness and vengeance which are not really in their natures. Neither the liberals nor the conservatives in the Republican party wanted Richard Nixon to be President, yet they had to take him because they could agree on no other, and one must say that he represented the only common denominator with which the Republican party had left itself: fear of the unknown. Nixon did not know his country, he did not like its people, and he feared both it and them. That above all was what Watergate told us, if we still had to be told it so late. Unhappily the Republican party may hide his portrait, but it has only to look in the mirror to find what are still its main features: the lineaments of a great political party that left its own country forty-five years ago, at the same time leaving the century. It has yet to find its way back and make John and Margaret feel at home in them both.

TWO

The
Donkey
Serenade

A President on the
Shoulders of His Party

JIMMY CARTER WAS ELECTED in the end because he was
able to stand on the shoulders of his party; if humility
came naturally to him, he might say with Isaac Newton
that he stood on the shoulders of a giant. This is not to
belittle him. In order to win, he had to climb onto the
shoulders of his party, which he did; and he had then to
make it stand up for him, which he just managed to do.
The party was there, he captured it, and it then carried
him. But he is not Newton, and may well forget this.

The Democratic party in this century: there are stories
to tell of it to one's grandchildren. One may laugh at it—
it needs to be laughed at. One may fear it—it is sometimes to be feared. But even its rivals, although they may
forbear to cheer, cannot refuse it the tribute of a reluctant envy; they have at least grudgingly to admire. It
is of its country—no party is more so; and of its time—no
party so much. And yet it can be such a donkey, such a
jackass. In 1976 it showed yet again that it is still the
normal governing party of the most powerful and most
restless free nation in the world; but it is hard to say
why for half a century it has deserved such trust.

Its record has been extraordinary. For almost fifty

years since 1932, it has held power—either in Congress or in the White House, or in both simultaneously—with such regularity that the few interruptions seem almost like deviations from the natural order. Only once in this time has it ceded to the Republican party the simultaneous control of the White House and the Senate and the House of Representatives; and even then it was for only two years. What is more, these have been years of pain and disturbance, almost of revolution, in which the character of the United States and the nature of its role in the world have both been profoundly altered, yet the Democratic party has remained.

It has been the maker of modern America, and to an important extent the maker of the modern world. One might use of it the words inscribed on Christopher Wren's tomb in St. Paul's: *Si monumentum requiris, circumspice:* "If you seek a monument, look around you."

Look around you, indeed! The country is not at ease, the world is threatening. What a monument! If the Democrats have been in power all this time, it would seem they have a lot to answer for. Whatever else they have built, they have not built a cathedral; and one must add of course that it is not one of the functions of politics to build cathedrals. But what concerns us is that whenever the American people in these years have turned to the Republicans, they seem to have been even more disappointed. With however much reluctance, they again lifted their ears in 1976 to the donkey serenade, almost fifty years old.

This has to be explained. Harold Macmillan once said that even when they were not in office the Whigs in Great Britain had in effect governed the country for two hundred years, from the Glorious Revolution of 1688, which they had engineered, until they left the Liberal party in 1886 on the issue of Ireland. What he was talking about was a governing class, what today we might call an Establishment. Although it is often tried, it is not easy to translate such terms to American soil. Nevertheless, at least something of the same may be said of the Democrats in the past half century. To recognize that they have been the normal governing party of the country is not quite enough.

It is not just to a party that the American people have

given such consistent authority in Congress, and which it has returned so often to the White House; and to which in 1976 it was ready to hand over the entire federal government, executive and legislative, and also a majority of the state governorships and legislatures. It is not just to a party that such a clean sweep is given, especially when that party shows all the signs of wear and tear, and even of corruption, after so long in power.

The Democrats may not represent a governing class; they may not be an Establishment. Yet when one says that they are of their country, and of their time, one is saying something of what Macmillan said of the Whigs. After all, if the Whigs engineered the Glorious Revolution to their own advantage, it can as well be said that the Democrats engineered the New Deal to their advantage. That does not diminish either the New Deal or the Glorious Revolution, but it at least gives us a starting point.

There is an important sense in which what America now is, is what the Democratic party has made it. In so far as politics is responsible for such things, the social and economic system of the nation and the general principles of its foreign policy have been of its making. A people needs to find a reflection of itself in one or the other of its great parties, preferably in both, for then it has a choice; and however shattered the glass that the Democratic party holds up to it, the American people still recognizes in it a reflection of its own self-image, even if it does so with a grimace and does not confidently ask: "Mirror, mirror, on the wall, who is the fairest of them all?"

We should not talk so much of the survival of the New Deal coalition that Roosevelt put together—for that coalition is shaky, if it can be said to exist at all—as of the persistence with which the Democratic party is still able to identify itself with the country that has emerged since the New Deal in ways that even it could not have predicted.

However hard one tries, it is difficult for even the most objective of observers, if such can be found, to write of the Democrats in the same terms as of the Republicans, for in the one case one is writing of success, however qualified, and in the other of failure, however incomplete. In the case of the Republicans, one is speaking of their failure because of themselves; in the case of the Democrats, of their success in spite of themselves. Our curiosity must be different.

If Jimmy Carter had to climb on a giant's shoulders to win in 1976, and then make it stand up, it has nevertheless to be acknowledged that it was a giant whose legs were sawn off at the knees. When it at last stirred itself to win, it was as if a circus dwarf had taken to the stump: a large head and a strong frame, but having to take three scampering steps to the winning post where once it would have taken a single stride. It only just made it, as in fact it had just failed to make it in 1968.

It was not insignificant that Carter chose to open his actual election campaign in Warm Springs, Georgia, the resort at which Franklin Roosevelt used to vacation. A party that can enjoy such a memory is fortunate; there is no comparable home of a previous president from which a Republican candidate would choose to launch his campaign; in fact, nothing was more striking in 1976 than the fact that the past president to whose image Ford tried to appeal was none other than Harry Truman. But a party with so strong a memory is also in danger. It will sing the same serenade as before, and lo and behold! enough of the electors were ready to listen. But what does it do when given power?

The Democratic party is almost dramatically holding its own as the normal majority party of the country after almost half a century. But as a governing party it is sadly uncertain of what it wants to do. What has been most clearly missing—in 1968 and in 1972, and again in 1976 —is any forcible conception in the Democratic party itself of what it would like a Democratic president to accomplish. It was not so much Carter who wavered in his campaign—any more than any other candidate, not least Roosevelt in 1932—but the party itself, which had nothing really to tell him except to sing the old serenade and rely on the state of the economy to make it sound as seductive as before.

A party is not only a coalition of interests, it is also a coalition of ideas, which must be made to cohere intelligibly and to be seen to do so. The Democratic party at the moment is without a public philosophy; and a governing party without such a philosophy is a danger both to the country it governs and to itself. It is very different to govern than it is to manage. To manage is merely to dispose, merely to arrange to get through without too much controversy or too many mistakes. But to govern is a political art in which imagination is brought to play, not merely to dispose of events, but to charge one's response to them with a creativity that is born of purpose.

Too much is made of the mere improvisations of Roosevelt and the New Deal, for behind them, apart from the humanity of Roosevelt's own purpose, were the convictions of a generation reared in a public philosophy that was in their life's blood. Out of the actions of that generation and that administration there came more than its measures, for good or for bad; there came also an imagery that inspired a nation to twenty years of creative and decisive purpose between 1932 and 1952.

A nation that is great in wealth and power needs to be great also in spirit. It needs to be given not only certainty of purpose but breadth of vision; and that in the middle years of this century was the doing of Roosevelt and the Democratic party. America came home to itself in the 1930s and the 1940s, to act with imagination and courage not only in its own country but in the world. It was led, and it led; and nothing is more urgent than a restoration of that spirit. It will be difficult: The mistaken manner in which John Kennedy tried to restore such a spirit—the too large expectations too extravagantly raised—and the tragedy and the debacle in which it ended—including many of the posthumous revelations of the methods used —have made doubters of many of those whom a nation needs most to believe.

One cannot talk of the Democratic party in this context as of the Republican party. Still clearly the normal governing party of the nation, the Democratic party has to be observed and addressed as if it is, in large part, the nation that it has had so large a hand in making this century, and potentially at least again a redeemer of that nation. One of the main hopes of the present Democratic administration must be that Jimmy Carter himself, coming from a region of the country with a strong imagery of its own, and with a long sense of history, will restore to politics the language of imagery that it needs.

At the Democratic Convention in 1972, while they listened to George McGovern give his acceptance speech, Eugene McCarthy said to Norman Mailer that McGovern was lacking in all sense of metaphor. A better critic of politics than he is a politician, McCarthy was correct in his observation. Politics needs an imagery and metaphor of its own, both to contend with the languages of the other realms with which it must wrangle and whose claims it must meet, but also so that ordinary people may know what the political activity is, and why they need it.

This is one reason why an examination of the Democratic party in the past half century must concentrate so much on the political character of its leaders. It is from them in the end that the imagery must come, that imagery then to enter the life of the nation; and there can be little doubt that one thing that disturbed many people in 1976 was the sense of the strength of the personal imagery that Jimmy Carter carried with him, like Joan of Arc hearing bells in her head. It was a long time since the country had been asked to entertain the idea of a leader with not only so powerful a personal imagery but so powerful a regional and historical imagery as well. Yet in office too much of the strength of that imagery has seemed to be dissipated.

Search for other reasons; the essential fact remains: Carter can be little if his party does not come spiritually to life, and if the restoration of its life is not an immediate and urgent part of his own purpose.

Taking Politics As
Its Mistress

WHATEVER ELSE MAY BE said of the Democratic party in this century, no one will deny that, at least until recently, it has enjoyed politics. It would not rather have been in business or in law, in medicine or in real estate. It has not been a church or a reformatory, a Sunday school or a Rotary Club. It has engaged in politics as much for the sake of politics as for anything else: for the game—the chances, the dangers, the defeats, the triumphs, the luck, the opportunities, the disappointments—and it has played it hard, never wearying of the routs or discomfitures, the rushes and rallies.

Politics has been its mistress, or its addiction, which may be saying the same thing. It does not pray, "Deliver us from temptation." It lives to be tempted: no pussyfoot it! Even now, the allure of politics draws it on—to it almost cares not where. If it is to perdition, then to perdition it will go, singing "Happy Days Are Here Again." No sinner has ever fallen through the circles of hell with so little complaint or foreboding, or with so much confidence that at the bottom of the pit it will find hosts of the damned it may command.

Prissiness is not among its faults. Even today one thinks

of it most easily in a bar, sawdust on the floor, a derby on its head, its thumbs in the armholes of its vest, a cigar in its mouth, aiming now and then at the spittoon but just missing it; and ready at the sight or sound of a Republican to leap to its feet and punch him on the nose. It has a taste for a donnybrook, like the Irish who are so much a part of it. The image is out of date, yet it still tells us something.

In some ways, the most important legacy left by Franklin Roosevelt to the Democratic party was his gusto. The memory of that gusto has been in its lifeblood for more than a generation now, since he died; and whenever it has seemed to begin fading, something of the purpose of the Democratic party has seemed to begin to fade with it. A patrician he may have been, but he was not really very far from that figure in the bar. The jutting jaw and the cigarette holder, the bellowing voice, which could so sedulously woo, the gusting laugh which could force tears, and the endless gossip, the ceaseless talk about political life, its "fights for the fearless, and goals for the eager": These were not very far from the saloon.

"At the cabinet meeting the President was in very good humor, continually cracking jokes," Henry Wallace wrote in his diary while he was vice-president; "nothing of real importance came up." Such stories are legion. Rayburn described him as a "terrific waster of time," and said after his death that when the "Big Four," the leaders of the Senate and the House of Representatives, had their meetings with him, Roosevelt "would gossip along saying not much of anything for an hour and a half." This was the same enjoyment in politics as might be found in a ward boss. The true politician expatiates about his profession day and night.

It is endlessly fascinating to him, and the reason is obvious. The raw material of politics is human nature—one might even say, it is human nature in the raw. Whether he is trying to move a mass of people or one individual in a smoke-filled room, the politician is always working with his own nature on that of others.

Roosevelt pitted his colleagues against each other, and watched and listened—and learned—as they disputed and fought, among themselves and often with him: holding the reins loose, and then sitting back, again to watch and listen—and learn—as the more mettlesome became entangled in the traces, or the plodders failed to pull their weight. He "often made a game of it." said Harry Truman; he "had a lot of fun while he was President. He could not get around very well, and it would stimulate him to watch others match wits." There was mischief in it, but there was also purpose: not only to divide and rule, not only to give those who served him territory from which to fight, but to test their natures.

Not everyone thrived in this atmosphere. In his diary of December 7, 1944, Wallace described Roosevelt's proposal to shuffle about some of the responsibilities within the administration: ". . . it sounds like one of the brilliant improvisations which the President so often makes in order to get out of a tight spot . . . [In] the process of improvising the President puts the person for whom he improvises in a position to step on a great many toes. . . . I think the President gets a certain amount of satisfaction out of improvising in this way, and then watching the results without shedding any tears but, in fact, with a considerable amount of satisfaction." Wallace was repelled by the method, especially when he was the sufferer; but also how much he admired.

On another occasion he grimaced at Roosevelt's manner: "The President is certainly a waterman. He looks one direction and rows the other with the utmost skill." But that is exactly what any politician worth his salt must do from time to time.

Always in Roosevelt it was done with gusto. As he teased his colleagues through one presidential term, and then through a second and a third and into a fourth, though a depression and into a war, what else was he doing but searching out their natures? At this level, government is a thing not of laws but of men. The exercise of great power is redeemed by the constant reminder of the human frailty of those who held it in their hands. It is the earnest and the unsmiling, like Richard Nixon, who let power puff itself up, swell like an evil toad, and do what it should not do. Power needs to be kept to a human level.

It is the humanity of Roosevelt that still throbs in every recollection of him. "The President is a fine companion to be out with," wrote Harold Ickes in his diary; "he can both recieve and give a thrust," and Ickes himself was not a diffident thruster. He spoke of Roosevelt's "ability to laugh and relax," and said: "I have never had contact with a man who was loved as he is." These tributes are all the more remarkable when we consider that they came from one of the most iracible men in politics; and their testimony is not diminished by the knowledge that as the years passed, and Ickes continued to serve Roosevelt, the relationship became more trying to them both.

But there is more even than that. Except perhaps in his exuberant vitality, Roosevelt was not other than the rest of us, and yet his humanity became an act of imagination in him as a politician, an act of sympathy with others whose circumstances could not have been more different than his own, and which cannot easily be explained.

A reporter who was opposed to the New Deal in its early years once approached a mill worker in North Carolina to find out what "that man" in Washington meant to him. The mill worker did not have to hesitate. "Roosevelt is the only man we ever had in the White House," he said, "who would understand that my boss is a sonofabitch." It is all there: all that ordinary people asked of him, expected of him, saw in him, trusted in him. At the beginning of 1934, Sherwood Anderson went on a tour of the United States, and a workman said to him: "There's Mr. Roosevelt . . . it's funny . . . I never heard anyone say whether he has any money of his own or not. . . . I guess if he was very rich they'd tell about it." Of course the worker had been "told about it," but what he was saying was that Roosevelt had been by some imaginative act transcended his own circumstances.

Someone once said that Roosevelt's polio was his log cabin, from which he rose to be president. Certainly there was *some* log cabin from which there came his imaginative sympathy with the sufferings of unfortunate people: a sympathy which, as Frances Perkins tells us, sometimes broke out in private into an anger on their behalf.

Accompanying it all was his enjoyment of politics, a belief that government could be used to improve the lives of ordinary people, and therefore that politics needs no apology. At a threatening hour in a fearful century, when madmen and bullies were strutting the earth, he made the government of free people seem possible and enjoyable; he made it effervesce when everywhere else it was flat in spirit. Most of the American politicians in this century who have exhibited that enjoyment have been Democrats.

It was characteristic of the Democratic party in 1976 that even those who wished their party to be returned, and wanted to support Jimmy Carter, looked for some story about the man that told them that he stayed up late to play poker, or sat up with the boys, or did anything that hinted that he had, as Ickes said of Roosevelt, "the ability to laugh and relax" which is "priceless to him and means a great deal to those who work with him."

They were looking for a nature to redeem the exercise of great power. After all, what was wrong with Nixon was that he was, according to the several accounts those who were familiar with him have given us, "happiest when he was alone with a yellow pad," calculating how he could win, always calculating something; and Carter in office has got to give the reassurance that he does not have the same fault.

It is inevitable that the Democratic party should have this concern. If it is to believe in big government—and it must believe in big government if it is to do the rest of what it believes ought to be done—it must be concerned about the characters of those to whom such government is entrusted. Somewhere along the line in recent years—the line that may be drawn from Roosevelt to Truman, and from them to Kennedy and then Johnson, its own four presidents—the Democratic party has learned to distrust the exercise of power and to distrust big government, and so has even seemed to lose something of its enjoyment of politics. Many of its doubts about Carter in 1976 reflected its own uneasiness with itself.

"It's a great game, thoroughly worth the playing," exclaimed Woodrow Wilson when he was governor of New Jersey. But he never really enjoyed the game. While he was governor, says one of the sympathetic of his biographers, he "revealed his temperamental inability to cooperate with men who were not willing to follow his lead completely; he had not lost the habit, long since demonstrated at Princeton, of making his political opponents into his personal enemies, whom he despised and loathed." Much of his difficulty with Henry Cabot Lodge—who was admittedly not the most agreeable of men—arose from his own lack of enjoyment in the game which he nevertheless said was "thoroughly worth the playing"; and in 1976 one could again feel people responding uncomfortably to what they believed to be intimations of the same temperament in Jimmy Carter.

We could only read in discomfort of the stag dinner which Wilson gave at the Trenton County Club for the Democratic and Republican leaders of the New Jersey Senate, to strengthen the majority for his legislative program: of the chicken and waffles, of the quips, of the three-piece band, of Wilson and one of the Republicans leading the company in a cakewalk, and of Wilson's own comment afterwards that "The rest of the evening was one unbroken romp. . . . The senators are as jolly as boys when they let themselves go." For this was not Wilson, and the story only draws attention to the fact that it was not, as if he would have liked us to believe that at college he had spent nights on the bottle with the ladies of the town.

His stiffness was more himself—William Allen White said that his handshake was "like a ten-cent pickled mackerel in brown paper. . . . He had a highty-tighty way that repulsed me. When he tried to be pleasant he creaked"; and the stiffness reflected an inflexibility of political will which in the end was disastrous: that inflexibility reinforced by the self-delusion, which he often expressed, that he was the voice of the people's will and ultimately of a will that seemed to transcend all limits.

Wilson greeted his nomination to be the presidential candidate of his party by saying: "I am a Presbyterian and believe in predestination. . . . It was Providence that did the work at Baltimore," where the convention had been held. Such a man is not confidently to be trusted with the exercise of great power. Moreover, he made this remark to William McCombs, who had done as much as anyone to engineer his nomination, and who said that he felt a chill run up his spine: "I stood there a complete wreck [from the campaign]. I saw other drawn faces about me. . . . I could not accept Wilson's view of foreordination."

The missionary impulse in the Democratic party is so strong, and it is by now so used to governing, that a human sense of fallibility and limit is one of the characteristics that it needs most in its leaders: a deprecatory and

self-deprecatory saltiness about the sometimes sublime—
for that cannot be denied—but as often ridiculous business in which politicians are engaged. The concern about
character during 1976 was the concern of a party troubled
about its own impulses.

The saltiness was there in Sam Rayburn as Speaker of
the House, and in a different manner in Alben Barkley as
the majority leader in the Senate, during the years of the
Democratic party's supremacy in the middle years of this
century. Even Henry Wallace could say that Barkley was
a "joy for ever"; and Hubert Humphrey has said that to
Barkley politics was, in the words of John Adams, "the
spirit of public happiness." If the techniques of oral history had been used in his day, he would have kept the
tape recorders running with humorous and illuminating
anecdotes about the life of politics. It was with this character that he carried the Democratic Convention in 1948
to its feet, and himself to the vice-presidency.

Maury Maverick, the Democrat from San Antonio in
Texas, may have been right that Sam Rayburn "would
sell out his grandmother if he thought that would again
make him Speaker of the House"; but that is not an ac-
cusation, made by one politician about another, that
would have caused Rayburn a sleepless night. He knew
the game, he played it hard, and he did not play it to
lose. In his office every afternoon, he held an informal
gathering of intimates and some members of Congress.
"It's time to strike a blow for liberty," he said as he
brought out the liquor, asking with a smile, "Why be stupid and weak when with one drink you can feel smart
and strong?" One must smile with him, with the irresistibly disarming way of the man, and with the unaffected
and wry admission that the exercise of power is in the
hands of ordinary and fallible men.

Harry Truman was of course an exemplar of this mode.
In fact, Truman in the White House, Barkley in the Senate and pulled from it to be vice-president, and Rayburn
in the House, together reflected the character of the Democratic party in mid century, an earthiness of spirit which
to some extent accounted for its unexpected victory in
1948. It was familiar to the people; it seemed to have
grown from the same soil as they.

Truman put up with very little nonsense from the self-important, because he was not self-important himself. "Feel free to attack me anytime you think it's going to help you back home in Minnesota," he said to Humphrey in 1952. "If it helps to kick me in the shins, go ahead and do it. It may hurt, but at least I know it's from a friend." Hardly had he become president in 1945 than Ickes sent Truman an abrupt note about something to do with the Philippines, and at last Ickes went to see him. "I want you to feel perfectly free," said Truman at the beginning of their conversation, "to come over here at any time and call me any kind of S.O.B. if you want to."

It was all in the character of the man; and again it was for some hint of this kind of character that many Democrats were looking in their candidate in 1976, and perhaps still look for in him in office. When everything else has been said of the 1948 election, was it not for this kind of character—as against that exhibited by Thomas Dewey—that the American people then voted, when every apparently sensible prediction, except his own and a few others, said that Truman must go down to defeat? Truman's mother-in-law may have wondered why he should run against "such a nice man as Dewey," but then mothers-in-law do not see their sons-in-law with an unbiased perception.

Following the early hagiographers, Hubert Humphrey has written of the "levity and banter" that characterized the Kennedy administration. "A presidency without that is grim," he says. "Without that, too easily can the man, a voice of the people in a democracy, become emperor, king, prince, or despot." He is right, but the Kennedy administration is hardly the best example to make his point. The levity was only levity, the banter only banter; and the way in which power was being exercised was not really questioned.

The men who engaged in them, including the president and his brother, were as imperial and kingly and princely, as earnest and exalted in their mission to the world, as any American administration in this century. What one misses in them is any evidence of humor. There was no saltiness in the administration. It was the first Democratic administration in this century that seemed far removed from the figure in the saloon, in his derby and his vest, and to be-

long to a new world of centurions and courtiers. In a way
that had not been true under Roosevelt or Truman, power
was exalted. It was exalted above the rough-and-tumble
of politics; it was made unpolitical. One of the reasons
the enjoyment of politics is so important is that the political life, with all its boisterousness and its distractions,
continually interrupts the majestic claims of great power.

Lyndon Johnson was trapped, not only by the war in
Vietnam but between these two worlds: the one of the
politician, the other of the centurion. He came from the
world of Truman and Barkley and Rayburn—less fortun-
ately he came also from the world of both Tom Connally
and John Connally—and as such he was "a big 'un,
Lyndon," as none other than Nicholas von Hoffman wrote
after his death. "We're going to miss you, you old booger."
Even those who had most severely criticized his Vietnam
policy could recall that "This was no ordinary human;
this figure was larger-than-life," as TRB put it in the *New
Republic*: recalling his office as the majority leader of the
Senate in the old Capitol as a kind of Sistine Chapel,
with allegorical nymphs floating around the ceiling, and
the banks of telephones and buzzers and speakers on his
huge desk, which he operated as if he was playing the
organ; and Johnson "fitted right in."

Everyone who met him has his own memories, and one
may tell one of one's own: of the evening when he called
a handful of foreign correspondents to the White House,
and long after he had ceased to invite questions from
them and they had put down their pencils and closed their
notebooks, he went on talking and reminiscing, gossiping
and telling anecdotes of the political game, interrupting
himself only to call Robert McNamara at home: "Bob,
I'm going to be late. You and Mary eat without me. I'll
bring a can of Campbell's tomato soup with me. It's all I
want"; and with that the President of the United States
resumed the instruction of his captive audience.

Humphrey himself tells how Johnson cajoled Harry
Byrd into reporting out the tax cut bill in the Senate in
1964. Johnson seized Byrd at the end of an annual Grid-
iron dinner, carried him off to the White House, plied
him with "giant fingers of Old Grand-Dad," called Lady
Bird Johnson down from her sleep to sit next to him in
her dressing gown, told him jokes and chattered into the

night, until Byrd, as Humphrey puts it, "the captive of an elixir that was part Old Grand-Dad, part Lady Bird, part Lyndon Johnson," gave his promise, and a few days later appeared on the floor of the Senate and reported out the bill.

That was indeed the apprentice of Sam Rayburn, at least as gifted a sorcerer as his teacher. But partly because of the manner of his succession, Johnson found himself (or at least allowed himself to be) stuck with men from outside the political world, such as Robert McNamara and McGeorge Bundy, and they were not men whose measure he could feel with his thumb. Humphrey adds to this point when he criticizes Johnson for his wish as president to make unpolitical appointments: "He took great pleasure in talking about how many civil servants he had promoted" to high-level political positions, "as though that would make him non-political." The truth is that, if Johnson had been more political as president, if he had remained the pupil of Rayburn and not the apprentice of McNamara, he might have recognized the quagmire into which he was wading: even if simply that he could not get away with it.

One of the purposes of the life of politics is to challenge the claims of power. Power is of course a part of its business, and power is drawn from its life; but politics also stands in opposition to power, reminding those who exercise it how fallible are the instruments, how weak the men, how untrustworthy the occasions; how the sand always shifts.

To some extent the Democrats are possessed by politics. "Politics, more than most other careers, requires constant attention," Humphrey has written. "Success requires monomania. Politics intrudes on and defines your life style." It is impossible to imagine a Republican using those words, and they tell us something of the party we are now describing.

When Truman was fifty years old, and was about to announce that he was a candidate for the Senate, he wrote a note to himself in a hotel room in the middle of the night: "It is 4 a.m. I am to make the most momentous announcement of my life. I have come to the place where all men strive to be. In reading the lives of great men, I found that the first victory they won was over themselves and their carnal urges." One thinks of the man and of the occasion, and reads the words again. Here is another Democrat who is to reach the highest office, confessing to lust in his heart, and to its repression. They are illuminating not only about themselves but about the nature of their party.

Sprung from the Loins
of Bosses

DURING THE SECOND WORLD WAR, when he was the British ambassador to the United States, Lord Halifax met Al Smith, and in his diary wrote of the "Happy Warrior" of 1928: "He was exactly like a rather elderly and demoralized bookie—brown billycock—and it is rather terrifying to think that he should have aspired to be President of the United States a few years ago." One wishes that one had witnessed the meeting between the English aristocrat, a pillar of Anglicanism, and the son of poor Irish Catholics, his father a boss truckman, born into what Herbert Croly called the well-developed and self-contained community of Tammany Hall.

By the time Halifax met him, Smith was old and embittered; he was not happy, and he was no longer a warrior. Even before 1932 his opposition to Roosevelt was not tempered, and before Roosevelt had been in office a year he denounced his monetary policy. "Al Smith has definitely aligned himself with the bankers and Wall Street," wrote Harold Ickes in his diary; and there was something more than a little sad in the later life of the man who, as governor of New York, had an (until then) unequaled record for social legislation and relatively honest and efficient government.

146

He deserves to be remembered best as the presidential candidate of a national party who when he went west of the Bronx on his campaign refused to abandon his emblem. "He came buoyantly down to the luxurious special train at Albany that night of departure," Thomas Stokes recalled, "and he had on a brown derby. So he was going to wear it after all." It was not only his emblem. It remains the emblem of the election he fought in 1928, at which the new immigrant working class began to rally to the Democratic party.

The election of 1928—where the story in this book may be said really to begin—has been analyzed at least as much, and probably more, than any other presidential election in the history of the United States. Smith lost four southern states, which had voted Democratic since the Civil War, but he hastened the historic new alignment of the urban working class in the North which is still, as was again shown in 1976, one of the basic facts of American politics. He ran far ahead of the congressional candidates of the Democratic party, and he piled up emphatic majorities in twelve of the largest cities of the nation, from Boston to San Francisco. Not just a symbol, he was the magnet.

Politics was in his blood, and it was in his belly, as it was in the bellies of most of the children of the immigrants in the cities. Politics fed them. "In my boyhood all men, young and old, leaned quite naturally toward politics. . . . Young men were prompted to be active for the purpose of securing political preferment. Political appointment gave them an income greater than they could earn for similar work in private occupations. . . . The neighborhood political club was always the center of political activity." To be a member of the police or fire departments was to be an ensign of the political machine, to be well-known in one's neighborhood, and to be given respect and to have influence in it. It was as intricate a social order as feudalism.

In 1972, George Meany could recall the same system: "Now in New York, where I was brought up, all we knew was the Democratic Party. I recall as a kid when there'd be baseball teams backed by the Democratic Party in my district. They'd be passing out Thanksgiving turkeys to people. You could go to the Democratic club. This was an area where there was a lot of poor people, although it certainly wasn't a slum. You could go to the Democratic

147

club every few weeks and get an order for half a ton of coal. And there were jobs. I remember the thousands of people we put on snow removal in the dead of winter. Five dollars a day for snow removal. Shoveling snow. Thousands of people."

This was Smith's world. Politics was its bricks and its mortar. As a boy he watched the torchlight procession that used to be a feature of election campaigning in the big cities, and which survived until recently only in the Chicago of Boss Richard Daley: the "long lines of men in the Democratic Party keeping step with the words, 'Blaine! Blaine! James G. Blaine! A continental liar from the state of Maine!'," the kind of lusty slogan for which a candidate would today be held to account by the prudish journalists recruited by the League of Women Voters.

He deserved the designation of the "Happy Warrior" at the time—one that could hardly have been given to the Democratic candidates who immediately preceded him, including Woodrow Wilson—and what one must notice in this, for it is far too often overlooked by political scientists as they run their statistics through the computers— is the interaction between a party and its chosen leader, when that choice has been true. For it was the Democratic party in 1928 that took the necessary risks for the sake of the party's future. One of its leaders at the time said: "It would be less embarrassing to accept Al Smith and risk the loss of the election than to turn down and alienate four million Roman Catholics in New York, Illinois, New Jersey, and Massachusetts."

When the Demcratic party had last won the presidency from the Republicans in 1912, it had been the result of a freakish swing of power to the South and West; but now it was ready to put both at risk. It was prepared to meet the taunt of Bishop Adna W. Leonard when he sent out his call to the "Nordic, Protestant, English-speaking world," asking it to vote against "Al(cohol) Smith" and his "wet, Tammany, Roman Catholic, Booze gang."

It is doubtful how important the Catholic issue was, and one of the most perceptive studies of the election is inclined to support the view of Herbert Hoover that Smith "would certainly have lost," had he been a protestant, "and might even have had a smaller vote." But what must interest us here is the Democratic party's sense in 1928 of a future it could then hardly have imagined, and the readiness of its leaders, not least those from the South, to take the necessary risks for it.

It may well be that Jimmy Carter's campaign in 1976 contained the same kind of sense of a future not yet fully imagined: that coming from the South, as half a century before Smith had come from the North, he sensed the possibility of a new alignment, which may again determine the frame of national politics for a generation to come. The groups that he just managed to hold together during his campaign, after the fragmenting of the 1960s, were as various as those that began to coalesce in 1928; and if Carter represents a new South, it may be as important as Smith representing the new immigrants, although he has still to prove in the 1978 and 1980 elections that the 1976 coalition was not a mere accident.

It is not hindsight to say that the Democratic party was ready to lose in 1928 for the highest stakes in the future. There is plenty of evidence that its leaders knew exactly what they were doing, and before Smith's nomination in 1927, an editorial in the *New Republic* put the argument into words: "He is quite the best losing candidate whom the Democratic Party could nominate. They might *feel* more like a real party after they lost with him than they would after they had lost or even won with any other nominee." The motive was not quixotic or purposeless. It was a deliberate response to the new forces at work in society that could find no opening into the Republican party.

The Democratic party as we know it even today was sprung from the loins of bosses, and many of them were sprung from the loins of the new immigrants. If the Democratic party took possession of the country in mid century, it was primarily because the new immigrants had arrived at the position in which they were claiming the country as their own. This is not the place to describe—to criticize or defend—the bosses and the machines. It is enough to say that the comparison with feudalism is not facile. Feudalism was a complicated system in which rights and obligations were exchanged for the mutual if not equal benefit of all those who were recognized to be in the system. The boss system at its best was something like that.

"Honest graft" was a term with a genuine meaning. Things got done, for people who needed them, in ways that were understood and accepted, by people who were expected and could be relied upon to do them. That is not a poor claim to be made for a political system, especially when there were no other institutions that would undertake the task.

When the cultivated French writer Bertrand de Jouvenel came to the United States, he was told that if he wished to know how the American political system worked he should talk to Tom Pendergast, the boss of Kansas City. Pendergast was leaving New York on the maiden west to east crossing of the *Normandie;* Jouvenel rushed to the ship and listened awestruck, as Pendergast explained to him: "It's a very simple thing when you come down to it. There's people that need things, lots of 'em, and I see to it that they get 'em. I get to my office on South Main Street at seven o'clock in the morning and I stay there when I'm in town till about six o'clock at night, and during that time I see maybe two hundred, maybe three hundred people. One needs a half ton of coal. Another woman's gotta get a job for her boy. I see to it that they get these things. That's all there's to it."

Well, it was not *quite* all there was to it! Pendergast made himself sound like a Robin Hood who had worked honestly for the fortune which he so lavishly distributed to the needy. But the greed of some of the bosses, the fact that "honest graft" all too easily slid into flagrant bribery, the misuse of patronage and payoffs, and the scandalous involvement of some of the machines in actual crime, do not alter the fact that the system performed a function that had to be performed.

But our interest is with the influence of the bosses and the machines on the character of the Democratic party. In the first place, they made one of the nation's great parties acquainted with the very streets of the cities that were then changing the face and the character of the country. Not only was rural society still strong in the United States until the Second World War, the rural image was even stronger. John Morton Blum has pointed out that, according to John Hersey in *Men on Bataan,* the men who followed Douglas MacArthur were all rural heroes: a captain who was "the product of the land, born of a long

150

line of pioneers"; a chaplain also of pioneer stock; a lieutenant who could never forget the farm on which he was born; and so on. What is more, this was true of other wartime novels. The small towns "won" the war.

The strength of this rural society and rural imagery was reflected in the political life of the nation: in the Populists and the Progressives, perhaps most vividly in William Jennings Bryan, of course in the La Follettes, in the overemphasis on rural society in the New Deal, and above all in the excessive influence allowed to the country as against the cities in the whole political system, an imbalance that has even now not been fully corrected.

It was in these conditions that the power of the city bosses in the Democratic party, able to deliver their millions of votes, helped to redress the balance at a time when it might have been a catastrophe if the cities had been denied their proper voice. It was the city machines that took the national party onto the city streets; and ever since then it is the Democrats who have been far more comfortable on those streets than the Republicans for whom these cities once were strongholds.

George Meany has vividly described what this meant in terms of the Republican party's failure to hold the cities: "Now there was a lovely avenue in that neighborhood [where he was brought up], the finest in the neighborhood. It had some three-story brownstones. One of these three-story brownstones was the Republican Club. I remember the green shades, and the initials of the club were in gold letters—I remember that. And those shades were never raised and nobody ever saw a sign of life in the club except on election night every two years, when the club would be lit up, especially for the election. And that was the only contact the people had with the Republican Party." Much of the political history of the country in this century is to be found in that memory of a man who has stridden it: "those shades were never raised."

The bosses and their machines forced the Democratic party on to the streets of the great cities; they also forced it to take in the new: not only the new, but the alien. Hart Crane was from Akron, Ohio, and when he revisited it in 1919 he wrote to a friend: "The place is burgeoning with fresh faces. . . . I saw about as many

151

Slavs and Jews on the streets as on Sixth Avenue." And that was only Akron. Across the Northeast and the Midwest they had spread, into the cities, there to find in the machines and the bosses an institution they could use to force their way into full citizenship, and through the machines and the bosses into a party that did not reject them, because it could not afford to do so.

The lack of exclusiveness of the Democratic party has been one of its most distinguishing marks in this century. When it began to scoop up the northern black vote in the 1930s, it was simply scooping up another lot of newcomers to the great cities. It did not keep out the black, because it had not kept out the Slav: a fact many Slavs were later to forget, when they had "made it," but which the Democratic party as a whole did not forget, because it could not afford to do so.

Out of the welfare activities of the machine there also came the welfare politics of the New Deal. Instead of distributing coal and a turkey, the Democratic party would distribute the jobs and the money with which to buy the coal and the turkey. One has already said that the Democratic party engineered the New Deal to its own advantage, as much as the English Whigs had engineered the Glorious Revolution to their advantage; and it had had good teachers in the bosses.

In 1935, the two senators from Missouri were Harry Truman and Bennett Clark. They joined in recommending to the federal government that Matthew Murray, as loyal a member of the Pendergast organization as could be found, should be appointed the director of public works in their state. It was the kind of request the Roosevelt administration found difficult to refuse. Four years later, when Murray was sentenced to jail for income tax evasion, after the collapse of the machine, it was estimated that $250,000,000 had been spent by the federal government on WPA projects in Missouri, and that at one time Murray had had no less than 142,000 people on his payroll. Beside these figures, it seems to be of only casual interest that Truman, when he became president, gave a full pardon to Murray. If there was anything that Harry Truman understood about politics it was that one good turn deserves another.

But there were intangible influences that the bosses

and the machines had on the Democratic party. With the extraordinary candor that runs through the whole of his invaluable biography, Hubert Humphrey tells of a lesson he learned while he was running to be mayor of Minneapolis. He says that "there were liberal aldermen who couldn't have cared less about helping," and he goes on: "This taught me early why loyalty and reciprocity are so valued by politicians. Cronies and retainers who slavishly surround a public man, sycophants chorusing his praise, may be disgusting and worthy of derision by outsiders. They may even be galling to the man himself. But in the highly competitive, all-or-nothing world of politics, where it seems there are always more people shooting at you than helping, loyalty, above all else, seems important." This is something that the bosses—our figure in his derby in the saloon—knew very well; and it tells of an attitude to politics as a pursuit in itself that is a part of what we have to explore.

For above all, what came out of the bosses and the machines, sucked from the streets of the cities, was a belief in politics as an activity in itself, without which the governance of modern society must be surrendered to even grosser powers. As we have seen, it was bred into Al Smith from childhood: "I had a choice of hard labor at a small wage of ten dollars a week, or twelve at the most, in the kind of jobs that were open to me, or easier work at a greater wage. I had a fondness for politics and I liked the excitement of public life. I had plenty of friends and I always took much satisfaction in helping them." In Humphrey's words, "loyalty and reciprocity" are at the basis of the political life.

Harry Hopkins knew as much: that gaunt and dedicated man, that most intense and yet practical of idealists. In his diary of November 15, 1944, Henry Wallace wrote: "[Justice] Murphy said that Harry Hopkins' idea of politics is to be able to get patronage for the big city bosses and to telephone them from time to time to get things done from their end of the line. . . . I told Murphy that I was aware of the fact that in 1940 Hopkins looked on the appeasement of the city bosses as the beginning of political wisdom." As the beginning of political wisdom, maybe, but hardly as the end of it, and what is wrong with Wallace's estimate is that he hardly seems to hear the import of those words: "to get things done from their end of the line."

The essence of the Democratic party in this country has been that it has wished "to get things done," and that in order to get them done, it has been ready to use every political institution in the nation to do them, "from their end of the line." As long as it did not try to circumvent the institutions that existed—even if they were machines and bosses—its readiness to exert the authority of the federal government to the full had at least a check, as well as a support. A great deal of the fear of Jimmy Carter in 1976 was the fear of a man, who having come from "nowhere," did not seem to be subject to any check or prompted by any inspiration outside his own circle, which he himself had created; and as he entered his second year of office this remained the main fear.

To be possessed by politics, as the Democratic party has been in this century, for good reasons and for bad, is only safe if there exist in the political system men to whom even a Harry Hopkins, one of the most intimate counselors of his president, must pay the respect of understood dues.

A Question of
Friendship

THE MAN WHO REALLY benefited from the nomination of
Al Smith was the man who put his name in nomination
at the Democratic Convention and gave him the title of
the "Happy Warrior." Memories are important to parties:
their futures are to some extent imagined from their pasts.
A whole half century of the Democratic party is caught
in these words of Hubert Humphrey, describing his
father's return from the 1928 convention:

"When Dad returned, filled with the drama of the convention, he poured out every detail of every speech, every
fight, every personality. He showed off his souvenirs as if
they were relics. . . . His identification with Smith was
extraordinary, but as he recounted events of the convention, he became even more excited about the man who
nominated Smith. . . . By the time he had finished reading
the news accounts of Smith's defeat [at the election] he
was already looking to the day when he could campaign
for Franklin Roosevelt."

It was remarkable that a drugstore keeper from a small
town in the Midwest should so identify with Al Smith,
pull out "his delegate badge, Al Smith posters, and a little
brown Al Smith derby made of cardboard," and then

"dash about the county trying to convince everyone that Al Smith was the man": a county in which the Ku Klux Klan burned crosses in 1928 to remind the people of the dangers of a Catholic as president, and which suspected a man who, as well as being a Catholic, was Irish into the bargain, a Democrat and wet. And it was no less remarkable that the same drugstore keeper should have identified even more strongly with the most patrician of the potential candidates for the future, who was making his return to national politics after his illness.

One again senses in the reeaction of Humphrey's father the extraordinary vitality of a party that had really not been the normal governing party of the nation since the Civil War. It is still very difficult to understand from where this vitality was coming, until one feels at last driven to suspect that it may just have been an impassioned movement of every drinker in the nation to get rid of prohibition. In fact, prohibition was a not inappropriate symbol of much else that was changing in the political climate at the time: of the machines whose operations were, to an extent not easily to be overstated, dependent on the generous lubrication of liquor; of the new urban Catholic immigrants who were in rebellion against the imposition of an established Protestant ethic; and of a working class that could hardly help observing that prohibition was a classic example of one law for the rich and another for the poor.

"The question of prohibition," it has been said, "was one of the underground forces undermining the old party alignments from 1922 to 1932," but it would be more accurate to say that it symbolized those forces; and by the time Herbert Hoover took office, it was not so much a matter of "leaks in the dike," as Denis Bogan has put it, as of "broken levees with the flood of booze pouring in like the Mississippi," and on that wave rode the new forces in American society. "The lesser breeds without the law" were wet even in North Dakota.

In 1927, twenty months before Al Smith was nominated, "Big Bill" Thompson was elected Mayor of Chicago. The election of a Republican boss was not exceptional and certainly not nearly as interesting as the platform on which he ran. He promised that "instead of ordering cops to break into the houses of good citizens and frisk mattresses for booze," he intended to send them back to their beats. This was understood to mean that the licensing of gambling and drinking privileges would be regulated by the payment of graft to city hall. As for the rest, he advertised his Americanism, defying any foreign monarch to try to participate in the government of Chicago, especially King George V who, poor man, as was tartly observed at the time, was not even allowed to participate much in the government of England.

Here was a Republican in a great northern city appealing to the class-conscious subcommunity of the new immigrants: people who danced a good deal, as they drank a good deal; whose lives seemed always to be stimulated by "some sport, some public festivity, some crime" in their neighborhoods; who were sometimes well-disposed to lawbreakers as they were also sometimes disposed to break the law themselves, since it was the established law of the old order that seemed alien to them; and who resented "the respectability, the alien conventions, the moral self-importance, and the exclusiveness of the descendants of the early settlers." They were a new force, and what still seems astonishing, when one considers the victory of Bill Thompson, is that on the national level it was left to the Democratic party to gather them to itself and, in doing so, to give them a hand up into American society. "American has Americanized them," it was said at the time. "They propose now to Americanize America."

They were rowdy and restless, gullible and violent. But it was Herbert Croly, liberal and intellectual, who in 1927 noticed something else about them. "What these newcomers have most craved from the older Americans is the extended hand of kindness, sympathy, good-fellowship, and equality. They or their parents, for many years after their arrival, lived lonely lives in strange and harsh surroundings. . . . They require, consequently, more than anything else in their political favorites, a sympathetic personality and the sense that he is playing the game with them." Into that yearning community came the figure of Franklin Roosevelt.

We are speaking of those who are now called "the ethnics," their parents and their grandparents; and before we explore their relationship with the Democratic party today, we must understand their situation then. The need for "kindness, sympathy, good-fellowship" was important. Too much has often made of the material inducements the machines offered to them, the coal and the turkey, important as these were. The greater inducement was simply "friendship." "On the whole, the gifts and favors are taken simply as an evidence of genuine loving kindness," said Jane Addams, the settlement house worker, at the beginning of the century; and half a century later, a precinct captain of the Democratic party told two social scientists: "After all, this is a question of personal friendship between me and my neighbors." That was as late as 1955.

It cannot be emphasized too much that it was this kind of "friendship" that was at the heart of the appeal that Roosevelt was able to make, to sustain for so long, and to leave as a legacy to his party. And one means at its *heart*. "Have a heart," said Croly in 1927, was one of the characteristics phrases of the new immigrants; and in 1932 they suddenly saw a man who "had a heart."

"I've been thinking," said a workman to Sherwood Anderson in 1934, who described himself as one of the "dead ones like me, the ones they can't use any more": "I've been thinking, from what I've read and what I've heard him say, that he gets the picture." One of the best journalists of the day, Anne O'Hare McCormick, wrote toward the end of the First Hundred Days of the New Deal that Roosevelt "is the kind of man to whom people talk frankly, to whom strangers write freely. Every day he receives hundreds of letters from obscure citizens in all parts of the country. Most of these letters require no answer, but they are put in his 'bedtime folder' and he runs through them every night or early in the morning."

In 1944, he was old and ailing; in fact, he was dying. Yet on October 21, he drove through four boroughs of New York in an open car in pouring rain. "Wet streets, sodden leaves, chill winds . . . so cold that we six reporters sat huddled together in our closed Cadillac," said one reporter at the time; but at the head of the cavalcade was the president, "rain streaming from his glasses and wind whipping down the sleeve of his upraised arm," even speaking in the rain to the crowds. Rain and cold in New York, rain and cold in Chicago, rain and cold in Philadelphia, and he did the same in each.

If this was gallantry—because he did not have to do it to win—it was a gallantry that told of his respect for the processes of a free country, for the ordinary people whose votes he sought, and above all for those very new immigrants who wanted to know of a politician that he was "playing the game with them," and yet from whom he seemed by birth and background to be so distanced.

We have got into the habit of thinking of the New Deal coalition as no more than a coalition of interests, blocs of voters put together by the material favors that were bestowed on them. But that is not the whole story. If it were, the Republicans would long ago have broken the coalition far more convincingly and less intermittently than thay have done. What was still at work in 1976 was the legacy of a man of an exclusive background who created a party that did not exclude.

For the coalition was not conceived and born at one election, or out of one mind, or by one method. The northern cities were not brought in at a single stroke. As late as 1935, Edward J. Flynn, the boss of the Bronx, was warning Raymond Moley that "There are two or three million more dedicated Republicans in the United States than there are Democrats," but that the population was drifting to the cities, and that it was in the cities that the new voters whom the Democrats needed were to be found. "They include racial and religious minorities and labor people. We must attract them by radical programs of social and economic reform." Hence the motive for the new radicalism of Roosevelt before the 1936 election.

Ed Flynn was one of the most intelligent, perhaps the most astute, of the modern bosses. Whereas the by then incompetent rulers of Tammany managed to put themselves on the wrong side of Roosevelt when he was governor of New York, Flynn became his supporter and his friend, and was later to be a frequent guest at the White House. In his own book *You're the Boss,* he described how he put together a slate in the Bronx: "Our ticket shaped up as well-rounded one; Lyons and Foley were Irish, Joseph and Lyman were Jewish, Delagi and Loreto were of Italian descent." He had learned well the lesson of Smith's success in 1928 in pulling into the Democratic fold not only the Irish and the Catholics but the Italians and the Jews. He had nice ways of describing the uses of patronage: "One can (and in the Bronx we do) frown on any attempt to influence a judge to commit an improper act without minimizing the part that personal friendships play in such matters as appointments."

He was a boss, urging "radical programs of social and economic reform" on the Democratic party in 1935; and in 1948 supporting Hubert Humphrey's fight for civil rights at the Democratic Conventions, with other contemporary bosses such as David Lawrence of Pennsylvania, Jake Arvey of Illinois, and John Bailey of Connecticut. Perhaps they gave their support to Humphrey because they wanted to attract the liberals and the blacks, labor and the other minorities; perhaps they needed something with which to hold off the threat of Henry Wallace from the left; perhaps they even just wanted to take revenge on the South which had deserted Smith in the end in 1928, a "get-even gesture twenty years later." But one cannot refuse Humphrey's own evidence: "As I came to know the party bosses better, I found that they agreed with the spirit, the principle, the rightness of our plank. They reflect a deep current running in the party and in the country."

What one is describing is a system in which it was known by everyone where power lay: not only by the president and his counselors in their wish to get things done by the bosses at "their end of the line"; not only by the Democratic party in its need to gather votes; not only by the liberals in the Democratic party who knew where the essential leverage had to be exercised; but also by the people themselves who could not be bought if the essential element of "friendship" was lacking.

The voters were not trapped, in either sense of the word, into voting for the machine. If it could not deliver what the voters wanted, it could not deliver the voters to the party. Flynn himself was to discover this when, in February 1948, his vacation in Florida was ruined by the news that his organization's Democratic candidate had been defeated in an election in the East Bronx by a young lawyer, Leo Isaacson, who was running for Congress under the banner of the Progressive party led by Henry Wallace. The most obvious explanation was that since the East Bronx was then 40 percent Jewish the vote had been a protest against Truman's policy at the time toward Palestine.

But as Samuel Lubell, one of the most acute of political scientists, pointed out, the East Bronx was then in a state of radical upheaval as a result of the influx of blacks and Puerto Ricans: It was not merely a Jewish neighborhood, but a dying one.

Whatever the reason, it was one of many demonstrations that the machines and the bosses had, by the time our story really starts, to keep their ears very close to the ground. One of the many errors of Tammany by that date was to oppose the nomination of Herbert Lehman to succeed Roosevelt as the governor of New York. This not only brought Roosevelt and Al Smith into alliance against it, but Lehman proved to be an even more successful vote-getter than they had been.

Since the collapse of the boss system—although there are still machines and bosses, and the relics of them—the Democratic party has been unable to replace it. There have been the unions; there is the federal welfare structure, which does more of the work of the Democratic party than is usually acknowledged, in ways whose consequences are either intended or unintended; and there is a widespread administrative class at the federal, state, and local levels that has to be regarded as a largely invisible arm of the Democrats. But there is now no institution attached to the party as efficient in vote-getting as were the machines.

But something else has not been replaced. The bosses and their machines were, first and last, politicians and not administrators. It was politics they understood, politics they practiced, politics they relished. Today the great danger in the working of the political process, and therefore to the Democrats as the governing party, is that politics will be replaced by administration. Contrasted with politics, administration is limited in its motives, confined in the influences to which it is subject, secretive in its methods, impatient in dealing with obstacles, undemocratic in its procedures; and above all, intolerant of the untidiness that is a part not only of free but of efficient government. The administrator simply would not understand what G. K. Chesterton meant when he sang of "The night we went to Birmingham by way of Beachy Head." He believes that the straightest route is the most effective. In politics it rarely is.

When one thinks of the administration of Franklin Roosevelt, one thinks of the hurly-burly of politics; when one thinks of that of John Kennedy, one thinks of the administrator's illusions of cost effectiveness. It is not that the presidency has become imperial that is the point so much as that it has become unpolitical. The association of the great city bosses with the New Deal, which was primarily a deliberate choice of Roosevelt himself and of James Farley, was important for reasons other than that it would have taken them years to create any other kind of machinery which would have enabled them to look forward so confidently to electoral success. It also meant that the presidency was kept political.

It was in the machines that the dedication of one's own life to the political life was most complete. It may be a long time since Martin Lomansey of Boston said: "They the voters are just my friends. I am with them all the time and that's what counts"; or since Commissioner Murphy of Tammany Hall stood beneath a lamppost to talk to all who wished or needed to talk to him. But it was not really at the highest levels that the dedication began or was most complete.

"A good precinct captain or ward leader has very little time for home life," it could be said only ten years ago; "he spends his evenings visiting his neighbors, doing chores at ward headquarters, traveling to and from city hall on errands, and talking politics." This kind of dedication among the lieutenants and the NCOs traveled to the top in politics, as it was also demanded from there; and it was part of the whole atmosphere of the New Deal, continuing diminished into the Fair Deal, as Roosevelt leaned heavily at times on Kelly of Chicago, Flynn of the Bronx, Hague of Jersey City, Crump of Memphis, and, for a time, Pendergast of Kansas City.

There were bargains of course. But one cannot ignore the sheer sense of politics and political energy that the bosses brought to the Democratic party at that time, as one also cannot ignore the genuineness of the political instincts that led them to support the New Deal. In a way it was at the very moment when their power was fading that their exercise of influence and power at the national level had its culmination. At the Democratic Convention in 1948, Hubert Humphrey was sitting with Andrew

162

Biemiller, waiting for the debate on their civil rights amendment to begin. Flynn came over to them and said: "I hear you kids have a minority plank on civil rights. That's what we need to stir up this convention." He left them, and sent runners to the floor to fetch Arvey of Chicago, Hague of Jersey City, and Lawrence of Pennsylvania; and each reaffirmed to Flynn their support for the amendment.

Those were the days when conventions were conventions, and a roll call of the states sounded like a summoning of the dukes in a play by Shakespeare: "Come, faithful Pennsylvania, to horse . . . and you, our loyal Massachusetts, lend us your arms . . . oh! doughty Illinois, be you this day without doubt doughty . . . and honest Texas, carry your lone star to affright our foe . . . you sweet California, comeliest of our lieges . . ." And behind it all was the system of exchanged rights and obligations.

When a precinct captain in Chicago in the mid 1950s was heard to complain that he had called on a voter on a Sunday afternoon, to find him with three newspapers on the floor, watching television, and the voter asked him, "What can you tell me that I don't know?," it was clear that something had changed in the political life of the country, and so gone out of the life of the Democratic party. The attempt to find a replacement is part of the story we have to tell; the election of 1976 was one more effort to find an answer, and not a very successful one.

Literate Liberals and Privileged Plenty

PART OF THE STORY to be told is of the persistent duel between what, for the sake of shorthand, we may call the regular command of the Democratic party and whose who, again as shorthand, we may call the literate liberals. The distinction is not hard or fast. There have been and there are those who stand in both camps, with at least their feet if not their heads; the regular leadership has never been monolithic, and divisions among the literate liberals are chronic. But the shorthand is useful, and it draws attention to a phenomenon that is confined to the Democrats. There is not the same kind of duel in the Republican party with the literate conservatives.

One of the curiosities of the New Deal, and of the years that have followed, is that it produced no significant body of social criticism of its own. Out of the Progressive era there had come the writings of men such as Herbert Croly and Walter Lippmann, Louis Brandeis and Walter Weyl, to say nothing of the socialist muckraking and pamphleteering of men such as Jack London and Upton Sinclair, W. J. Ghent and William English Walling. Even in 1955, the historian Richard Hofstadter had looked around to see what comparable social criticism had emerged as a result of the New Deal, and could find nothing but the earlier work of John Kenneth Galbraith. Twenty years later still, we now look around and find nothing but the middle and later work of John Kenneth Galbraith. As far as radical criticism of the society is concerned, this is a case not of putting all one's eggs in one basket but of putting all one's water in one sieve.

But the New Deal at least also had the inspiration of such writings at the beginning of the century as those of John Dewey and Thorstein Veblen. This does not mean, of course, that the New Deal followed their analyses or prescriptions, but that it was informed by them: by the message that was both explicit and implicit in their works, that society could be more intelligently and rationally organized by rational planning and the experimental techniques of science. Another influence came at the same time from Harvard Law School, where a revolution was wrought, which proclaimed that the law was not a static body of precepts but a man-made instrument of social change. Even the "frontier thesis" of Frederick Jackson Turner was pressed into service: His history might celebrate the virtues of the rugged individualism of the frontier but it also seemed to proclaim that with the closing of the frontier those virtues were now out of date and perhaps improvident. In a famous speech he gave to the Commonwealth Club before his first election, even Franklin Roosevelt seemed to have absorbed much of this public philosophy.

But Roosevelt was not a theoretician. In a characteristic answer to a questioner who pressed him to define his political philosophy, he said merely: "I am a Christian and a Democrat"; and indeed what greater assurance could there be than that of being saved from eternal damnation, in the next world and in this? He was a politician, the most brilliant of improvisers; and the New Deal was consequently a series of brilliant improvisations. The usefulness to him of the young men whom he brought to Washington was not that they were socialists or planners but that they gave off ideas, as a reporter put it at the time, "like showers of meteors." His attitude to these ideas seems to have been an almost Darwinian belief that in the rough-and-tumble of politics the fittest would survive. And the atmosphere in Washington was one of rough and tumble.

Of the young New Dealers, David Lilienthal said that "we have seen them develop a kind of Phi Beta Kappa Tammany Hall." But then Lilienthal's whole life has been a series of experiments in administration and rational planning, with little comprehension of politics.

In this climate, the task of the literate liberals was clear, at least to them. They would develop a consistent criticism of the New Deal from the left, reinforcing in so far as they could every tendency in it to more rational planning and greater government intervention in the interest of what they presumed to be the common good. John Maynard Keynes might write to Roosevelt in 1933: "You have made yourself the trustee of those in every country who seek to mend the evils of our condition by reasoned experiment within the framework of the existing social system"; but it was exactly the value—and the values—of that system that they called into question.

Roosevelt might carry water on both shoulders, as Lippmann put it, proclaiming in a single speech in 1932 both that the public demanded "plans for the reconstruction of a better ordered civilization," and that "the American system of economics and government is everlasting." But the literate liberals would try to empty the second bucket, and keep the first one fuller than otherwise it would be. To say that they were, in the 1930s and the 1940s united by a common philosophy would be to stretch a point, but they were joined by a common attitude; if not by a common gospel, at least by a common text or two.

There is no way of telling what the New Deal or, for that matter, the Fair Deal would have been like without the pressure of criticism that they sustained. The voice of the literate liberal in the Democratic party can never be ignored. It may often be reedy; it is never altogether without impact. But the point that concerns us here is that until, say, the end of the 1940s, the literate liberal had a political stance. In however vague a way, he was a collectivist. Moreover he also had a day-to-day political purpose. "Mr. Roosevelt is now, as always," said I. F. Stone in 1944, "just a wee bit to left of center." The task of the literate liberals was to make sure that the Democratic party and he stayed there.

In 1976 it was no longer clear that the literate liberal

had any public philosophy or political stance at all; and it was difficult to know what it would now mean to say that he stands, and would like the Democratic party to stand, even "just a wee bit to left of center." In pursuing the decline of the political force of the literate liberal as a part of our story, we are exploring one of the reasons why the Democratic party today awaits a sense of purpose from it knows not where.

One of the persistent faults of the literate liberal is that he is a poor judge of character, and certainly of political character. Literacy is unfortunately often a temptation to vanity: to a sense of one's own intellectual and moral superiority, which one then transfers to a politician who seems to embody one's own tastes, one's own predilections, and one's own articulacy. Literal liberals often sniff: Their persistent fault is to surrender to men who they think smell like roses.

By the end of the 1930s, the liberals were persuaded that the New Deal was embattled inside an administration that was increasingly conservative. They needed a leader round whom to rally, they sniffed, and before long they had found what they wanted in Henry Wallace, "as earthy as the black loam of the corn belt, as gaunt and grim as a pioneer." Roosevelt chose him to be vice-president in 1940, then to drop him four years later. The battle was joined.

When the literate liberals find an acceptable leader, it is not enough that he is a politician; they must make him out to be more than a politician. They cloaked Wallace in many mantles: He was a mystic, he was a moralist, he was a visionary, he was a prophet. They gave him "The kind of devotion," as Lippmann wrote in 1944, "which Bryan and the elder La Follette aroused." One of them found in him "a curious blend of hardheaded practicality and an attitude of wonder at the workings of a God who makes the rain to fall and the corn to grow up out of the earth for the nourishment of man"; and God had sent him to them, to lead them out of the wilderness. Wallace shared their conviction.

But he was also a schemer, perhaps not an efficient one, but nonetheless a schemer. This is not as worrying to a literate liberal as might be expected. He affects a disdain for politics, yet he likes the aroma of power in his nostrils. He is reinforced in these attitudes by the high-minded schemer who carries the tittle-tattle of the political world to those who will applaud him, seeing how lonelily he contends with the evil that is around him. Wallace's diary is one long screed of telltale bitchiness. This may not matter in a diary such as that of Harold Ickes—which revealed a man who "could not possibly be as bad as he seems," said Richard Rovere: "selfish, vindictive, suspicious, servile, and disloyal"—but it does matter in a man who set himself up as so righteous, and disinterest-edly dedicated to the public good. Wallace enjoyed poli-tics, but his enjoyment was always advertised by him as the selfless effort to fulfill some divine revelation. In fact, he enjoyed politics only when he won, and he therefore in the end lost.

His vanity was at times impenetrable. One has to read only his own diaries, his own evidence, to see that Roose-velt warned him, again and again, during 1943 and into 1944, that he would probably not be the candidate for vice-president for a second term. Yet such was his capac-ity for self-delusion that when finally he was not chosen he could claim to be surprised and accuse Roosevelt of deception. Roosevelt played the game better, but they were both playing it.

In fact, Roosevelt warned him even against his naïve and increasing entanglement in the communist line toward the end of the Second World War, the entanglement that was eventually to be his downfall. When on March 13, 1944, Wallace told the president that he did not wish to go on his scheduled trip to Siberia and China unless he could do some good, Roosevelt answered: "Oh, you must go. I think you ought to see a lot of Siberia." Only a man as consumed with vanity as Wallace would not have felt the sting in that flick, and understood why it was a con-venience to Roosevelt to have him out of the country while he prepared to choose his nominee for the vice-presidency.

The political character of the liberal needs always to be studied with especial attention, because it is far too easy for him to persuade himself and others that his motives are of the best, and his conduct the purest. The same kind of vanity that enabled Wallace to record every bit

of tittle-tattle in his diary also led him to indulge in con-
tortions of self-deception in his defense of Soviet policy at
the end of the Second World War and in the years that
immediately followed. His sophistries were as contempt-
ible as he was contemptuous of any fact his arguments
could not accommodate. In the end, he earned the most
abrupt of dismissals even from Eleanor Roosevelt, who
had for so long been his admirer and ally. Underneath
that shock of hair lay a vanity that was so consuming that
the Progressive party he chose to lead in the 1948 election had only one sure support: the Communists.

When he announced his independent candidacy, he was
rejected by the Roosevelts, and by every other prominent
New Dealer. Even the left-liberal newspaper *PM* in New
York opposed the new party, and the *New Republic* un-
derstandably insisted that he had forfeited the title to
the independent editorship it had earlier bestowed on him,
although it was itself hardly a model of intellectual
straightforwardness at the time. The blacks did not go
with him, and the unions did not go with him, not even
the CIO. He was left with the support of the Communists,
and of course of a scattering of those literate liberals who
were as capable of self-delusion as their high-minded
leader.

It is worth studying these two passages from his diary.
On December 11, 1942: "After cabinet meeting which
was the shortest we ever had, I showed the President my
December 28 speech. He liked it but said that in view
of the fact that I was giving it over the air, he thought it
would be wise to reduce the amount of philosophic discussion dealing with the nature of liberty and equality."
And on March 4, 1943: "My proposed March 8 speech to
the farmers . . . The President would like to see me inter-
ject short choppy sentences, designed to wake up the
audience, even though the sentences may be rather unfair
in the context." The smirk of self-righteous superiority is
characteristic; and one must realize that it was not naïveté, let alone sincerity, that caused his downfall but the
vanity that set him above the advice of others.

But his concern with his speeches is important. The literate liberal is always overimpressed by articulacy, by the
verbal skills on which he prides himself: from Henry Wallace to Adlai Stevenson to Eugene McCarthy to Morris

Udall. The oratory of Wallace was of course very different from the skeptical and even almost ironic voice found by the following three. Wallace came out of his time and place, the Bible in one hand and hog prices in the other, to call into being what he insisted on referring to as "Gideon's Army." But it is the willingness of the literate liberal to be seduced by rhetoric, whatever its manner, that is so illuminating in those with such pretenses to sophistication.

What we must notice in all this—for it will recur in our story—is the preoccupation of the literate liberal with what in the 1960s came to be called "style." It is style in an almost literary sense to which they responded in Stevenson and McCarthy and Udall; and it was style (rather than his substance) that drew them at first reluctantly and then headlong to John Kennedy. We must explore this later, but it is the persistent heresy of the literate liberal to give to style in politics an undeserved significance. More than anyone else, he goes to politics for theater, for a theater of rhetoric in the old sense. Of all people, he is a sucker for a good line.

The style of Henry Wallace had its impact at the time because, as we have said, the image of rural society was then still strong. In the 1920s and the 1930s, in art and literature as well as in politics, there seemed to be a hope that some purifying influence would return from the Midwest, to reinform the East. Moreover, as a result of his agricultural researches, Wallace seemed to join the traditional values of a purer America to the new promises of technocracy, a word that was fashionable at the time. And this again is interesting, because it is an insistent effort of the literate liberal, however much he may be unaware of it, to try throw a bridge between traditional values and contemporary society. The literate liberal in the cities he would never leave is nevertheless hopeful that somewhere "out there" a fresh wind will blow across the prairie and refresh the contaminated life of urban America.

It is not an accident that Wallace came from Iowa, Stevenson from Illinois, McCarthy from Minnesota, McGovern from South Dakota, Udall from Arizona. The literate liberal yearns for a voice that will speak to him of a yesteryear of innocence still unbetrayed.

But there were of course the literate liberals in the 1940s who rejected the appeal of Henry Wallace, and it was they who formed the Americans for Democratic Action. As one turns over the pages of the *ADA Journal* now, sere and brittle to the touch, a faint odor of lavender and old lace wafts through the main reading room of the Library of Congress, and gray-haired men and silver-haired women at their desks lift their heads for a moment, like deer in a pasture, as if they have scented something on the wind they recognize.

But it is only a memory. Nevertheless the memory is strong. At height of its influence, which was considerable, ADA represented the last occasion when the literate liberals in the Democratic party did not disdain the blue-collar workers and in fact felt with them a genuine community of interest. The alliance with the unions that ADA formed was not only an alliance of convenience. It grew out of a time in which the literate liberals had not completely escaped into the upper-income bracket.

They were on their way there, but the feeling that there was an identity of interest between them and the lower-income groups was still strong. Richard Hofstadter had remarked in 1955 that the New Deal had created a vast bureaucratic structure that was engaged in the kind of problem-solving that demanded professional skills, but it was the next generation of the professions that found the affluent society had lifted them on to the slope that leads upward to social and economic privilege.

We will see the importance of this when we discuss the attraction of Adlai Stevenson for the literate liberals. But at the end of the 1940s, those of them who were anti-Communist and members of ADA still instinctively acknowledged that the unions and the working class were their allies. As Hubert Humphrey was to say, "old New Dealers" were now "new ADAers." ADA might hold its convention in a fraternity house—as symbolic a setting as could be found—but at its conventions and out in the field of electoral politics, it worked closely with such unions as would cooperate with it. Walter Reuther of the United Automobile Workers was prominent at its charter convention; and the ADA cooperated in Michigan, not only with his union but also with the AFL. In Massachusetts a United Labor Committee was formed on a statewide ba-

171

sis, which brought together the activities of ADA and both the AFL and the CIO. As Humphrey built his power in Minnesota by first working to merge the Democrats with the Farmer-Labor party, and then driving the Communists and pro-Communists out of it, "Phil Murray, national president of the CIO, was the person who could help, so I flew to see him," and at the same time "We began organizing ADA chapters, too, as an additional method of finding people whose political philosophy was liberal but anti-Communist." In fact, on the national level, ADA played some part in bringing about the eventual merger of the AFL and the CIO.

But even the literate liberals in ADA, for all their effectiveness in organization in those early years, had some of the faults of their kind. They could not find the virtue in Harry Truman in 1948, and in their search for an alternative candidate in that year came alarmingly near to endorsing Dwight Eisenhower. "They felt that their politics were purer and their ideas better than those of Truman's people," Humphrey has commented, himself soon to become the chairman of ADA.

In 1952, when Lyndon Johnson was seeking to be minority leader of the Senate, and clearly could not be defeated, the group of ADA Democrats in the Senate decided to offer at least a symbolic resistance. "At that stage in American liberalism," Humphrey has again said, "it seemed important to have a symbol, even if you lost with it. Some liberals feel the only way you can be truly liberal is to take a position that cannot possibly succeed, and then go down with the flags flying. With that view, you are never so happy as when you are unhappy, and you're never quite so unhappy as when you succeed." Although wishing to engage in politics and in the struggle for power, the literate liberals were developing habits that were later to confound them.

The trouble was that they were ceasing to have any common public philosophy, especially one that was based on a coherent analysis of the post–New Deal society. In the foreword to *The Vital Center,* which he published in 1949, Arthur M. Schlesinger, Jr., one of the founders of ADA, said that he was persuaded that "liberals have values in common with most members of the business community," an unprovocative remark in its way and yet a far cry from the liberal accent of the 1930s. At almost the same time, John Kenneth Galbraith was arguing in *American Capitalism* that the process of business consolidation created within itself a "countervailing power" that mitigated the consequences that were previously feared. These were hardly the banners to excite a single-mindedness of purpose.

We will see later exactly where such policies led. In the second edition of his book, which he published in 1962, Schlesinger made a bow to Galbraith, and then said: "The problems of the New Deal were essentially quantitative problems—problems of meeting stark human needs. . . . Most of these are now effectively met for most Americans; [but solving them] only increases the importance of the quality of the life lived. These qualitative problems seem next on the American agenda."

He announced an "impending shift from quantitative to qualitative liberalism"; and in effect this means that the economic system is no longer open to any fundamental challenge. In his 1962 edition, he bowed not only to Galbraith, but also more deeply than before to American business: "I have more confidence now in the intelligence and responsibility of businessmen who have thought about problems of public policy." This is a liberalism that has been emasculated. It is also the liberalism of a professional class that has begun to indulge itself in the fruits of privilege. Such a liberalism might indeed be called effete; one might even say that it is Eastern; certainly it is Establishment.

The Influence
of the Unions

WHY DID HARRY TRUMAN win in 1948? Why does the paperback *Give 'Em Hell, Harry* sell round the nation? Why can that paperback then be turned into entertainment? In short, why should he be a folk hero, so that even Gerald Ford, running as a Republican, tried to invoke his name in 1976?

It cannot be the record of the man. His record was not all that distinguished. One must even be doubtful whether it can be just his character. His character was not all that prepossessing. He could be a cantankerous S.O.B., as he would himself have put it. He was not the embodiment of high ideals, or the promoter of great initiatives. It may have something to do with the times in which he ruled: times of unusual danger for the country, for which there was no precedent. Those whom we think of as the greatest presidents have usually been made by the great occasions they had to meet. Truman established the postwar security of the United States on principles that still generally apply.

But in the end one is forced to say that Truman is a folk hero in part because he was so representative a figure of his party. Truman was a Democrat. No one could doubt that he was a Democrat: to be detested as such by some, to be relished in the end by others. This relationship between the character of the man and the character of the party is of crucial importance in the forming of a popular judgment. Most people simply do not have enough evidence on which to judge the man himself, and so they look at him in relation to his party. He is a Republican or a Democrat, he has a record as such, his relationship with his party will to some extent dictate what he will do in office: All of that is at least a beginning for making a judgment, and people still await in Carter some evidence of the nature of his own relationship with his past.

"I was a New Dealer from the start," Truman later wrote of his first term as a senator. "I had been a New Dealer back in Jackson County, and there was no need for me to change. I believed in the program from the time it was first proposed." How much he believed in it we have already seen, in the record of the massive amount of federal money that poured into Missouri. He may have been an offspring of Pendergast, but the Pendergast machine had supported the New Deal from the beginning also, and no senator voted more loyally for the New Deal measures than Harry Truman. This was something by which the man could be known, not least when he proposed his own Fair Deal in 1948.

It must be remembered that the benefits of the New Deal—and of the abundantly productive economy that had been generated by the Second World War—were still comparatively new and could still seem precarious to millions of ordinary people in 1948. They needed a man they could trust not to dismantle the structure, and when he proposed a Fair Deal, however little of it might be enacted, he was in fact giving a promise that the past achievement was safe.

His success in 1948 had an effect on the Republicans. It was yet another warning—from the voters that they did not wish all that had been gained in the previous sixteen years to be taken away from them. If Eisenhower confirmed the New Deal by his administration, we cannot be sure that it would have been similarly confirmed if the Republicans had won under Thomas Dewey in 1948. What the voters would not risk with Dewey then, they were ready to risk with Eisenhower in 1952.

Many people who sensed in 1948 that Truman might win after all did not then thrust their own judgment. When Denis Brogan was covering the elections as a British observer, an eminent American journalist who was traveling on Dewey's train told him that having been on Truman's train it looked as if the president was drawing the larger and more friendly crowds. But he loathed Dewey so much that presumed his prejudices must be leading them astray, since the polls said otherwise. Although the *New Republic* at the time was a vehicle of Henry Wallace's opinions, even after he left the editorship, its political columnist felt the pull toward Truman in the country. "President Truman throughout 1947 has had one secret weapon, the GOP Congress," he wrote in January 1948, and three months later: "Frankly and candidly, we think Harry Truman is liked."

He was liked, and he was liked in part because he was a Democrat and a New Dealer. When Lyndon Johnson became president, he sought the counsel of Harry Truman, who told him that "a few of the big voices would try to drown me out from time to time, but the duty of the President was to lead and champion the people's causes." And again: "Harry Truman used to say that 13 or 14 million Americans had their interests represented in Washington, but that the rest of the people had to depend on the President of the United States. That is how I felt about the 35 million American poor. They had no voice and no champion. Whatever the cost, I was determined to represent them."

One cannot refuse this evidence, any more than one can ignore Johnson's own tribute to the particular contribution Truman made: "After the upheaval of World War II, the desire to relax grew strong once more. President Truman, who perceived the need for social change in the United States as clearly as any leader in our history, had to fight this apathy throughout his administration." It is the creation of attitudes of mind as well as legislative achievements that counts in politics.

R. A. Butler, a liberal-minded conservative politician in postwar Britain, once talked of "the patience of politics." One often felt as a politician, he said, that one accomplished very little of what one wished to do. But as the years passed one found that initiatives that had been begun and then seemed to fade had in fact "been working underground all the time." This was the real importance of the Fair Deal which was proposed by Truman in 1948. He was working on the mind of the country.

Congress may have thrown out his civil rights legislation, his national health care program, his proposal for federal aid to education, his farm legislation, the new public power project which he wanted, and his proposed repeal of the Taft-Hartley Act. But what mattered even more was that when next there was a Democrat in the White House the domestic program of John Kennedy drew heavily on the inspiration of the Fair Deal, and much of the genuine accomplishment of the Great Society in the 1960s was, as Lyndon Johnson was the first to admit, a realization of what Harry Truman had urged on the nation in the 1940s.

When one says that he worked on the mind of the country, one means in part that he worked on the mind of his party. Great parties are the repositories of all their past wisdom and follies; they store things up. The appeal Jimmy Carter eventually found that he must make in 1976 stood in the direct line of the New Deal and Fair Deal and Great Society. Eventually it was because he was a Democrat that he won, and recognizable as a Democrat, and he will forget this at his peril.

Truman enjoyed politics in the Democratic tradition. Everyone knows that the notice "The buck stops here" stood on his desk. But on the bookcase in the Oval Office there stood another motto, written on cardboard:

> If the trumpet sound an uncertain note
> Who will prepare himself for battle.

It was typed in black, except that "uncertain" was typed in red. There was much of Truman himself in that motto, but there was much else also of the party he led. Its zest for the battle, the gusto which Franklin Roosevelt had bequeathed to it.

At the first Cabinet meeting Truman held after Roosevelt's death, Henry Wallace found him "very vigorous, decisive, and hard-boiled": how decisive and hard-boiled he was to discover when Truman sacked him. At the same time. Taft wrote to a friend that Truman was "a straightforward man and much franker than Roosevelt. He has a quality of decision which is a good thing in an executive." But a great part of that decisiveness and that vigor came from the sheer enjoyment of the game. In no president in the past half century has that enjoyment been more evident than in Truman.

He "got away with murder"; he rewarded and he punished; sometimes he forgave, at least if it was a friend. When he succeeded to the presidency, David Lilienthal said that the reaction in Washington was one of "consternation at the thought of Throttlebottom, Truman. The country and the world doesn't deserve to be left this way"; and Edward Stettinius, then the Secretary of State, asked the other members of the Cabinet: "What would happen? Would there be another Harding regime?" And indeed there was enough scandal in the Truman administration to excite even the most diligent moralizer. Truman played politics as he had learned to play politics, and as the country then expected politics to be played.

He used the political system as it then existed, as he knew it, and as it generally was accepted. But he was not a corrupt man. He was probably fortunate that when he was a county judge the Pendergast machine in fact ignored the county level of government. His record as judge was immune to criticism. He used to say that Pendergast never asked him to do a dishonest thing, and a journalist who followed his career closely in Missouri said: "The most likely explanation is that the Kansas City boss knew it would do no good to ask it."

He made his national reputation in the Senate as the chairman of the Special Committee to Investigate the Defense Program—what came to be known as the Truman committee—and no one at the time or since has ever questioned the energy and skill with which he pursued every evidence of waste and corruption in the war contracts. One businessman who held contracts which ran into hundreds of millions of dollars went to Truman to persuade him to "call off his dogs." When he came out he was defeated and dishevelled. To every lengthy explanation that he had tried to give of his corporation's conduct, he had met from Truman only the question, repeated and then repeated: "Are the charges true or false?" It might well have been a one-man committee.

There was no socialism in his attitude to business, not really even any coherent attitude to the economic system. He disliked monopolies, and he disliked privilege; and above all he disliked the ordinary American being taken for a ride by big business *or* big unions. He would use the federal power—investigative or executive—to meet particular grievances against individual corporations or unions. But he was not of the mind to question the system of which the grievances were symptom.

The simplicity of his responses was both his strength and his weakness, and one thing he lacked we have already noted: There was no liberal left in the Democratic party by that time with a coherent social criticism to drive him and the Democratic party into taking a serious look at the economic forces against which the public power seemed able to contend only fitfully, in the series of executive responses to the crises which were one of the marks of his administration. This was never more evident than when Henry Wallace and the Progressive party made their challenge. Except on foreign policy, there was no fundamental difference between the challengers and the challenged. The Democrats were without a left.

The 1948 election was the last occasion when by its own organized effort the trade union movement in the United States played an emphatically significant role in the election of a Democratic president. That does not mean, as the election in 1976 demonstrated, that a Democrat can now win without the organized effort of the trade unions. But whereas the unions are today only a part of the support that a Democratic candidate needs to be elected, in 1948 they were more than their numbers. They helped to determine the character of the campaign.

In neither the Democratic platform in 1932 nor in Roosevelt's own speeches as a candidate was there any explicit appeal to the union vote. Throughout the 1920s, in America as elsewhere in the world, trade unionism had been weakened, and it apparently did not even enter the mind of Roosevelt or his advisers in 1932 that any particular effort was required to attract the organized labor vote. Perhaps no greater change was then wrought by the New Deal than that in the position and role of the trade unions.

When Roosevelt took office, the membership of the AFL had fallen to 3 million; the unions were strong in only four industries—the railroads, printing, the building trades, and the theatre; there was an open shop in the automobile industry; the coal strikes and railroad strikes of the 1920s had been failures; the migration of the textile industry to the South with its low wages only emphasized the general weakness of the unions; sweatshops were common; child labor was increasing; and with the Depression the whole wage scale had collapsed. It was not good, in 1933, to be a worker—man, woman, or child—and the unions were in no position to help.

If there was one political impulse that Roosevelt felt deeply, it was that it was a part of his obligation as a "have" to do something for the "have-nots." He was also a keen examiner of election results, and he could not help observing that in 1932 the most obvious division was between the "haves" who voted for the Republicans, and the "have-nots" who voted for him and the Democrats. He and James Farley were never ones to throw away blocks of votes which were for the taking. One could have expected, therefore, the kind of policies which Frances Perkins introduced at the Department of Labor. She would abolish child labor, and she would abolish the sweatshops; she would find ways to give the worker more pay and more security; she would insist on unemployment insurance; she was not interested only in higher wages and shorter hours.

All of that and more could be expected. If the 1932 election meant anything at all, it meant that the "have-nots" had arrived to make their case, and that they had elected someone who would hear it. But what was not inevitable was that not merely the working man as an individual but the trade unions as a movement would be brought to the center of the stage. Under the National Recovery Administration, the trade unions were given the right to life and liberty, if not obviously to the pursuit of happiness. The guarantee of the right of collective bargaining, and the challenge to the open shop and the company union, were measures which changed the dynamics of American life, and of the Democratic party.

Union lawyers such as Donald Richberg, who became the counsel of the NRA, and politicians such as Robert

Wagner, who had already sought the support of the unions, and became chairman of the National Labor Board, of course counted. But in fact Wagner represented something more. He had sprung from the loins of bosses, another protégé of Commissioner Murphy, yet he seemed to sense that as the immigrants began to take their place in society as Americans the boss system must decline, and that the workers and the poor would need a new institution. What the New Deal instantly recognized was that the unions were that institution.

At the election of 1936, it was not just the "have-nots" as individuals who voted for Roosevelt; it was organized labor, which lined up behind him with impressive force. John L. Lewis even joined with Sidney Hillman in a Non-Partisan League which gave $500,000 to the Democratic party, and provided an army of volunteer workers in industrial areas. Lewis especially appreciated the labor provisions of the NRA. With their help, he could restore his union and restore his power in it. The machines and bosses who were giving their support to the New Deal were in fact having their throats cut by it. The union organizer did not have to wait under a lamppost to meet his constituents.

As early as 1934, Sherwood Anderson perceived what had happened: "The New Deal has cracked something open. In the South and pretty much all over the United States there was, before Roosevelt came, a feeling that to have anything to do with a union meant a certain social blight. 'Not me. I do not intend to stay down there. I'm going to rise in the world.' President Roosevelt has, by recognition of the possible value of labor organizations, torn a door open." The Democrats had found another institutional basis for their power in the great cities.

In recent years, attempts have been made to suggest that the electoral power of the trade unions between 1932 and 1948 was not as great as was once generally believed; and it is probably true that the Political Action Committee of the CIO, especially, exaggerated its own influence as a result of various circumstances that told in its favor and of some striking individual victories in which its efforts seemed to be decisive. But it is not just by the numbers of voters, or the size of the funds that were distributed, that the influence can be measured. Labor gave the

Democratic party a spearhead, which was at least as important as the armies of voters that it was supposed to be able to organize, and to a significant extent did organize. They gave the Democrats a sense of direction, pointed them to where the needed voters could be found, and perhaps above all provided them with a sense of their own raison d'être. Until 1948, the main influence of the trade unions was to persuade the Democratic party that it was the party of the "have-nots" against the "haves," and that the "have-nots" needed their own organizations just as the "haves" had theirs. "The mass of voters have a perfect right to their own organization," said a sympathizer with the PAC in 1944, "which can contend for power with [the] reactionary and corrupt interests" that were already organized. That was the argument, and it was made to become surprisingly true in fact.

But the association of the unions with the Democratic party was never simple, and by 1946 the postwar inflation was driving a wedge between them and the Truman administration. They resisted the continuation of wage controls and were embittered by Truman's threat to draft strikers. But with a stroke of the pen, he was by 1948 able to bring them back into line, when he vetoed the Taft-Hartley Act. But not enthusiastically into line: The main effort of labor went into congressional and local elections, and most of these candidates they supported in fact ran well ahead of the presidential candidate.

In the 1950s the unions became increasingly conservative, but that is a later chapter in this story. The fact is that since 1932 the unions have existed as an institutional force in the Democratic party as they have never been able to establish an equivalent force in the Republican party; and more than any other single factor, this has affected the characters of the two parties as we know them today. For this reason, if for no other, the two major parties are not the same. The influence of the unions, and the need for the organized union vote, has held the Democratic party to the gut economic issues that still determine the lives of millions of ordinary people. When the Democrats have displaced those issues from the center of their concern, they have lost at elections, and the unions have turned to look elsewhere; and it is only the stubbornness of the Republican party that has prevented them from staying elsewhere.

But the continuing power and influence of the unions are not to be found most vividly expressed in presidential campaigns. It is in the successive election of Democratic congresses that they make themselves felt, and in state and local elections. There is where the unions hold the Republicans in check, and pin down the Democrats by the short hairs. But since these elections are a part of the working of the whole political system, they leave their mark on the presidential campaigns. The information that reaches an alert presidential candidate comes from many sources, both inside and outside his party, and the information that reaches him from the union-supported Democrats in Congress or in state legislatures or in city councils is hardly to be ignored; or if it is ignored as it was by George McGovern in 1972—when a union leader said, "He is having his own party, and I have not been invited"—the only possible result is catastrophe.

It was the old issues of the economy and inflation, jobs and taxes, which ultimately pulled Jimmy Carter to victory in 1976, and it is the keeping of those issues to the fore that is the function of the unions now, as it has been since the New Deal and the Fair Deal. In short, the unions present a persistent reminder to the Democratic party, and to the Republicans if they also would listen, that the "middle class" to which they appeal is still only on the margins of the affluent society.

The Prophet of the Politics of Affluence

ON THE EVENING OF January 22, 1952, Harry Truman asked Adlai Stevenson to take the nomination of the Democratic party; if he wanted it, he could have it. But Stevenson said No!—even though we now know from his papers that he was seriously calculating his prospects. Jake Arvey, the boss of Cook County and an astute politician, later said that Stevenson's casual reply had angered Truman: "He couldn't understand it. How a man could dillydally around with a thing like the presidential nomination." But for months Stevenson dillied and dallied, baffling and even irritating his friends and supporters. As one of the closest of them, Carl McGowan, later said, looking back on 1952, "When the mysterious tide that carries you to the presidency sets in, you had better go if you want it."

Stevenson sought the nomination of his party three times; he won it twice, and when he lost the third time, he did not much like the losing. He cannot be excused on the grounds that he was not ambitious. His ambition was marked, and the fastidiousness with which he seemed to pursue his ambition is less than convincing.

In each of his bids for the nomination, he confused his supporters and friends, and misused his party by his indecision. In 1953, Eleanor Roosevelt told him that winning a presidential election was hard enough, "even when one had the will and the drive; and that without them, it was impossible." Five years later, when the possibility of a third nomination was being canvassed, Truman recalled that before his first nomination Stevenson had been "too busy making up his mind whether he had to go to the bathroom or not." And behind the indecision there was always the self-delusion, the waiting for a draft, for a call: a listless prophet waiting for a chariot to carry him heavenward.

"If there's a touch of destiny about the draft business, then I don't want to thwart it," he wrote to Alicia Patterson on June 26, 1952, and eight years later he was writing to the wife of Thomas Finletter: "That I will accept a draft—yes—who wouldn't or couldn't!" The refrain is the same, played on a clarinet without a reed. He might ask the cup to pass from him, but oh! how he wished his party to press the cup to his lips. Eisenhower was watching the acceptance speech in which Stevenson prayed that "this cup might pass from him," and he later said "Right there I snapped off the TV set and said, 'After hearing that, fellows, I think he's a *bigger* faker than the rest.'"

It is hard not to agree with the general, especially when we now know that Stevenson had to ask for the biblical quotation—which one would have thought was rather well known to a literate man—from Dorothy Fosdick, who sent it to him, not intending it for a speech, but only to help the man make up his own mind.

Stevenson may have been a good man; that is not the issue here. His voice was one which needed to be heard in America in the 1950s; that is also not the issue. He simply was not fit to be the national leader of a great party. He did not even like electioneering. He said that campaigning for the presidency in 1952 was "a continuous and disquieting menace to equilibrium." It is a nice phrase; one can even sympathize a little with his repulsion, as one could sympathize with it in Eugene McCarthy. But in the end one cannot sympathize with a politician who does not like to be on the stump.

Speaking in the basement of a veterans' hall in the Midwest in 1952, Stevenson talked of the "disingenuous dissembling of the Eisenhower administration." It is again a

nice phrase, one would have liked to use it oneself, in a
letter to an aunt. For there is nothing laudable in such
insensitivity to a political audience. On the contrary, it
tells us that this is a politician who will not bother with
those whose votes he seeks by using a language to which
they can respond.

Yet the generally upper-income, professional, literate
rather than intellectual, liberals of the 1950s took him to
their bosoms. We must admit that the literate liberals have
a hard time. Their consciences are precious, in more senses
than one; and yet the aroma of power, like a perfume by
Halston, wafts about them, seductive and clinging. How
can they reconcile the two, their consciences and the
yearning for power. Their concern is almost theological:
how to make angels dance on the pinnacle of the Washington Monument. One knows them, and one reads of
them; and the moments of their caring are for albums, the
petals of violets pressed between the pages. The literate
liberals face choices from which common people ignobly
retreat. Eternal flames are lit in their hearts for the heroes
they choose, and then are extinguished by their tears as
they reach to another hero. Their consciences are tender
for losers, and envious of winners.

But we must place Stevenson in his time. With the decision of Harry Truman not to seek reelection in 1952—
a special provision had been written into the Twenty-
second Amendment to the Constitution to enable him to
stand—the period of the New Deal–Fair Deal came to an
end. Boss politics was being undermined by social changes;
union politics was more precarious than seemed on the
surface; and even as Truman won in 1948, there had been
hints of a change.

A number of New York Democrats who lived in the
Ninth Assembly District of Manhattan formed the Lexington Democratic Club to challenge the dominance of
Tammany. By 1953 they had achieved the election of a
district leader who was not a nominee of Tammany; and
by 1955 the direct election of district leaders had been
established. What might now seem to be only a local development was symbolically important and to prove of national significance.

The bosses in the northeastern cities were all being
forced into retreat: Carmine de Sapio in New York, Frank

Hague in Jersey City, James Curley in Boston. The liberal-labor coalition in the Americans for Democratic Action represented something of the same kind of middle-class movement, although with differences that were important. But above all, there suddenly appeared on the national scene a prominent figure who could be hoisted by the reformers into the national leadership of the party. The banner of the literate liberals was to be inscribed with the name of Adlai Stevenson.

But the story of the Lexington Democratic Club —which the club considered important enough to celebrate with its own historical account in 1959—is most interesting today because it foreshadowed the growth of exactly the generally upper-income, professional, literate rather than intellectual, liberals who have exerted such an exotic influence on the party ever since. They liked to believe that their affluence and position put them above the politics of patronage; that they were more interested in issues than in tactics; and that by a combination of reason and grace of spirit they would regenerate the country and fit it for its mission in this century.

Stevenson was important to them, both because he seemed to represent in himself all these attributes, and because his two defeats then enabled them to construct a rationale for their own dispirited sense of the futility and the vulgarity of politics in a democracy. Many of them would rather have lost for a third time with Stevenson in 1960 than have a chance of winning with Kennedy. Their slogan seemed to become: "You know when you are defeated that you are right."

This was a new upper-income professional class come into its own, the forerunners of the radical chic of the 1960s. They were far removed from the haberdasher's store of Harry Truman, or for that matter from the drugstore of Hubert Humphrey. They were also removed from the kind of memory that had made the Democratic party in this century, of union leaders such as David Dubinsky, who during the Depression had been unable to pay the rent on an apartment in the Bronx, or of Walter Reuther, who worked a thirteen-hour shift at eight-five cents an hour. They were not troubled with material insecurity, and not needing any institutions to protect them, did not place much emphasis on party organization or loyalty.

Political scientists and sociologists have since tried to label them: "amateur democrats," according to James Q. Wilson; "purists," according to Aaron Wildavsky; just "middle-class" to Leon Epstein, which is so vague as to be meaningless. By the late 1960s and into the 1970s they were all over the country, but mainly in the political clubs of the Northeast and the West, but also in some affluent suburbs. One political scientist who studied them in 1972 said that they were also to be found in some affluent suburbs, were college educated and upper income, were preponderantly young and heavily Jewish, and that they had a "distrust for party organization, disdain for regulars, and distaste for party loyalty"; but a "high regard for verbal skills." They are now familiar.

But there is more to it than that. "Adlai was never a real liberal," according to George Ball, who worked closely with him; and Stevenson himself complained in 1952 to Ernest K. Lindley, the Washington editor of *Newsweek,* that a story about him in that magazine "unfairly portrayed him as more liberal than he was." He kept his distance from ADA, to the point, as one of its leaders said, "where we were quite angry"; but with that little stamp of its feet, ADA lay down at his.

At a crucial meeting with a representative of Harry Truman in 1952 he said that he was opposed to the principle of public housing, that he would not repeal the Taft-Hartley Act, that he was not in favor of federal aid for education, that he was opposed to what he called socialized medicine, meaning Truman's national health care program, that civil rights were the responsibility of the states, and that the federal government ought not to put the South "completely over a barrel." In short, he repudiated the Fair Deal. Yet the literate liberals were championing him. Moreover, the conservatism of his views was only a part of the eccentricity of his position as a liberal leader of the Democratic party. His whole "life-style" in fact suggests why he should have become such a hero to the very people whom we are discussing.

When he entered politics in Illinois, his supporters were "drawn largely from the lawyers and financial men of LaSalle Street, from Lake Forest and other Northern Shore suburbs, from old college friends, and from the

Council on Foreign Relations"; and his sympathetic biographer adds that his circle, "not labor unions or ethnic groups or Negroes or other of the Democratic coalition, was the Stevenson base." Although warm in their personal support for him, they persistently regarded his political activities as something of a lark, like going on a picnic, as they did, with hamburgers and champagne.

Many of them were also Republicans. As one of these lifelong friends, Jane Dick, has said of them, they felt their "responsibility to society—it was not exactly noblesse oblige, but something like that, the idea that we who were so lucky had great obligations"; and she added with a touch that tells it all: "I thought it was romantic that my uncle proposed to his wife on a cracker barrel in Hull House." Unmistakably in that feyness is something of Stevenson's own voice.

In all of this Stevenson was an ideal spokesman for the literate liberals of the 1950s, who in growing numbers, as we have seen, were by then ceasing to perceive the problems of the country in economic terms. It even needed Michael Harrington to rediscover for them in the early 1960s that there was such a thing as poverty in the Galbraithian affluent society. For a time they got excited about poverty, especially about black poverty, but not for long. The poor are always with us, they might say, but they are not invited to stay.

The kind of political concerns that began to make their emergence in the support for Adlai Stevenson are those of a privileged upper middle class and their children. By the end of the 1960s and into the 1970s, the literate liberals were flirting with what was called the "new politics." The text of this new politics was provided by Fred Dutton in 1971: "The key political struggle of the decade could well turn out to be as much over the nature of our culture as the politics of the 1930s were over the nature of the economy"; and in that struggle the lower-income workers, unless of course they were black, would be the enemies, for they would not ally themselves with the sensitive concerns of literate men.

This is extraordinarily similar to Arthur Schlesinger's statement twenty years before that the liberalism of the future would be qualitative and not quantitative, concerned with "the quality of life" and not with jobs and pay envelopes. But politics that is concerned primarily with "the nature of our culture" is in fact the politics of an upper middle class that is secure in its affluence and its privileges, and has ceased to be able to imagine the condition of those less fortunate.

The difference between Adlai Stevenson and Franklin Roosevelt is that they both came from privileged backgrounds—Roosevelt's much more so than Stevenson's—but that Stevenson did not escape from it in his imaginative life as Roosevelt did, there to respond to the sufferings of others. Stevenson was always quivering with his own anguish at his own indecision; one never really hears in him a voice of pain at the suffering of others, it was pain at his own suffering, none the less real, but still limited. In the phrase that Ernest Bevin made famous, he hawked his conscience round the world, asking someone to set fire to the faggots beneath it at the stake.

After the 1952 election, Senator Burnett Maybank of South Carolina said that he and Senator Byrd would form a kind of triumvirate at the head of the Democratic party. "What about Stevenson?" he was asked, and he replied, "Oh, I never did hear much about Stevenson." The story is not just acid, for it tells a lot about Stevenson's relations with his own party. As one has said, it was not as if he did not aspire to lead it. After both his defeats, in 1952 and 1956, he tried to keep his hold on the party, and what is interesting is the method by which he tried to do it, the kind of people through whom he sought to remain the leader.

A year after his defeat in 1952, he wrote to Thomas Finletter, asking him if he would organize a group that would try to create a positive and appealing policy for the Democratic party while it was in opposition. One of the interests of Finletter to us is that he was a founding member of the Lexington Democratic Club. The kind of people he recruited came from the same kind of circle, and they took their task with some earnestness. They were irritated by the double insult that they were regarded as a group working only for Stevenson, while Stevenson himself did not apply himself with any very great diligence to the papers they produced. But they pursued their work, and were important in retaining the image of Stevenson as the natural liberal leader of the party.

Eight years later, after his second defeat, he was still the titular leader of the party, and he gazed with fondness on the Deomocratic Advisory Council set up by the party's national committee, of which the chairman at the time was of course a Stevenson nominee. For lo and behold! who was recruited to the new body but Finletter himself and very much the same people whom Finletter had enlisted to serve on the earlier group. The old Finletter Group had become the new Advisory Council, provoking from Harry Truman a denunciation of the "self-appointed guardians of liberal thinking."

There can of course be no place for such a body as the advisory council in an American party while it is in opposition. In the absence of a president, a more than titular leader, it must immediately seem to stand in his stead in opposition to the congressional leadership. But the point to us here is that Stevenson was ambitious to retain his own leadership, even unto a third election, but that the fastidiousness with which he chose to do so inevitably led him to associate primarily with a small group of the literate liberals, mainly in New York and Cambridge, who always seemed to spring from the mind of Thomas Finletter: his brainchildren, so to speak, and with no power base in the party at all.

Not only with no power base in it, but in fact with disdain for the places in the party where power really lay. For who were these "self-appointed guardians" but the representatives of a newly privileged class, in some ways the main benefactors of the society that had been created in part by the New Deal and in part by the huge productive capacity generated by the war? Whatever its other value, their voice has been one that has limited both the concerns and the appeal of their party.

In a phrase that anticipated another he used in his acceptance speech in 1950, Stevenson told an ADA dinner in 1950 that Roosevelt "knew that at the time he became president he was . . . the one man who could mediate between the old epoch that was dying and the new one coming to birth." Yet it was exactly this kind of mediation in his own time of which he seemed to be incapable. There is of course not all that much a defeated candidate and the titular leader of an opposition party can do, but he can do something, as was shown by the single campaign of Al Smith. He can assist in the redefinition of the party.

With the single exception of attracting the literate liberals of the upper middle class, Stevenson did not alter the relationship of the Democratic party with any signficant group in the country: not with the South, not with the blacks, not with the unions, not with the blue-collar workers. The party John Kennedy seized in 1960 had less identity than that which Harry Truman had handed over in 1952. It emerged from the Eisenhower years with self-respect, but with little else to show for its years in the wilderness, except that a new mode of political activity had been given a legitimacy within the party under the leadership of a man who was indeed an exemplar of it.

Jimmy Carter was first nominated and then elected in 1976 with almost no association with, or support from, the literate liberals we have been discussing. Some of them with their eyes on the main chance, when it began to look like the main chance, gave him help. But in general his victory seemed to mark the first emphatic defeat of the Lexington Democratic Club and its descendants since it was formed almost thirty years before. But this did not extinguish them. As Carter formed his administration, even he drew heavily from among them.

At the end of the 1960s, John Kenneth Galbraith asked in the title of a book, *Who Needs the Democrats?* The question now seems to be, Who needs John Kenneth Galbraith?

We can be certain that he will find his own answer, but it would be healthy if the Democratic party had more clearly decided than Carter seems to have done, of others as well as Galbraith, that their day is done. The good that these men did may live after them, but now is the time for them to rest in peace.

The Blacks: Poverty
by Another Name

ACCORDING TO HIS OWN account, Lyndon Johnson believed in 1960 that "a Southerner could not, and probably should not, be elected" to be president of the United States. In 1964, when he was already the president, he told his assistant, Walter Jenkins, "I just don't think a Southerner is a man to unite this nation in this hour." He had told James Reston of the *New York Times* that one reason "the country could not rally behind a Southern President was that, I was convinced, the metropolitan press of the Eastern seaboard would never permit it." He mentioned the reaction of the press to "my style, my clothes, my manner, my accent," and then said that he "was also thinking of a more deep-seated and far-reaching attitude—a disdain for the South that seems to be woven into the fabric of Northern experience . . . an automatic reflex, unconscious or deliberate, on the part of opinion molders in the North and the East."

Twelve years later, a Southerner was elected, but Johnson's words emphasize the significance of the achievement; and their truth was confirmed by many of the attitudes to Jimmy Carter in the North and East. Part of the distrust of him was and remains a distrust of the South.

The story of the Democratic party's relationship with the South, since Al Smith forfeited four of its states to Herbert Hoover in 1928, is one of the most extraordinary in the entire political history of the country. Smith himself recorded in his autobiography that at the Democratic Convention in 1924, "only one man south of the Mason and Dixon line ever voted for me in all of the 103 ballots." Since then the South has had every cause to escape from its allegiance, but in the end it has not chosen to do so. The failure of the Republicans finally to break the Democratic party's hold on the South is one story; the success of the Democrats in just retaining that hold is more than merely the reverse of it.

It was not difficult for Franklin Roosevelt to retake the South, and it was not very difficult for him to keep it. Ellis Arnall, formerly the governor of Georgia, might complain in 1943 that the North had turned a "great part of our country into colonial appendages and make the people of the South and West inmates of gigantic almshouses." But at least life in an almshouse is subsidized, and into the South during the New Deal there poured as much federal funding as was needed to sustain the dominance of the Democratic party. The South might be worried about economic policies that seemed designed to benefit only Northern industries, but the political subsidizing of the South was something that Roosevelt seemed to take as a political given. Why should he not spend some of the northerner's taxes in order to preserve in the South a political structure that helped to sustain an administration so attentive to the northerner's own interests?

The strategy worked during Roosevelt's four elections, and in 1944, the national committeewoman from Alabama told the Democratic Convention that "next November down South, it's going to rain and probably snow, but it won't be Dewey." But with the death of Roosevelt and the end of the war, the strains which had been increasingly felt at least began to pull too tight to be endured.

As far as the Democratic party itself is concerned, by far the most important decision was taken in 1936, when the national convention of the party eliminated the two-thirds rule for the nomination of presidential candidates. The story of the South within the Democratic party since then has been in part the story of a distinct region of the country, more or less essential to any Democratic hopes of success in a presidential campaign, deprived of its power to veto a nominee of the party, and yet not strong enough to secure the nomination of its own candidate. That the South endured for so long, and in the end with so little bitterness or resentment, a position of such inferiority in a party that was electorally beholden to it is one of the more remarkable facts of contemporary American history. Its economy was being dislocated, its culture was being disrupted, its mores were being threatened; and yet in the end it stayed.

The excellent political journalist of the postwar years Helen Fuller wrote in the spring of 1948: "Harry Truman may go down in history as the President who reorganized the Democratic Party structure. . . . [He] may inadvertently bring about the Southern 'purge' Franklin Roosevelt did not live to accomplish." She was referring specifically to the report of the President's Commission on Civil Rights, with its condemnations of lynching, of the poll tax, and of discrimination in employment and in education, all of which it proposed should be dealt with by federal legislation. A few months later, the Democratic Convention passed with the president's approval the historic civil rights amendment.

The Dixiecrats walked out, but the extraordinary fact is that the Democratic party knew what it was doing, as much as when it nominated Al Smith twenty years before. Nothing was more noticeable, for example, than that Herbert Talmadge in the last stages of his campaign for the governorship of Georgia began to soft-pedal the issue of racial supremacy. Sixteen years later, Lyndon Johnson was to tell a meeting in New Orleans of this period, when the ailing Senator Joe Bailey, born and raised in Mississippi and representing Texas, had said to Sam Rayburn: "I wish I felt better, Sammy. I would like to go back to old Mississippi and make them one more Democratic speech. . . . Poor old Mississippi, they haven't heard a Democratic speech in thirty years. All they ever hear at election times is 'Nigger, Nigger, Nigger.' " But as Talmadge sensed, the cry of "Nigger" was ceasing to pull.

This was a party that knew its South. Nevertheless it remains astonishing that in 1948, when it seemed to be fighting against every odd, and when it was already threatened by Henry Wallace from the left, it was ready with the support of its leader to risk the defection of the South. Of course the Democratic party was bidding for the votes in the great northern cities, but it is still hard to withhold admiration from a party which was ready to risk its Solid South for its future.

Into the breach it had opened went the Republican party under the popular figure of Eisenhower, and he broke the Solid South in 1952, and broke it even more in 1956, in spite of Adlai Stevenson's almost ardent courtship of it. Stevenson wooed it so intensely and so graciously that even the liberals who supported him were moved to protest. In 1956, John Sparkman was nominated as a southerner for the vice-presidency; the civil rights platform was qualified, which is another way of saying that its teeth were drawn; and no one was happy, except possibly Stevenson himself, whose naturally conservative inclinations must have hoped to find a naturally conservative support in the white South.

After all, it was he who said in 1952 that race problems would be more easily solved if the NAACP stayed out of them; and his friend Jane Dick warned him in a letter in the same year that "400,000 Negro votes lost in Chicago could be too many!" He did not like the decision of the Supreme Court in *Brown* vs. *Board of Education,* ordering the desegration of schools, and he said that "I get a little amused by the Northern liberals who damn us for making friends with the Southerners whom they seem to consider all conservatives." Unhappily the word "amused" is all too telltale. In preparation for the election of 1956, he courted the South more intently than ever. He tried to win over congressional southern leaders such as Lyndon Johnson and Sam Rayburn, and a segregationist such as Herbert Talmadge, and his irritation with young northern liberals who only "want to hear about civil rights, minorities, Israel, and little else" was difficult for him to repress. The 1948 decision of the Democratic party might almost not have been taken.

But the South was changing, more than Stevenson and many others realized at the time, and it needed one more shove, one more adamant exercise of the federal power, to push it over its own hump. That shove came in the mid 1960s from the Kennedy-Johnson administration. One puts it in that way because John Kennedy was reluctant until shortly before his assassination to grasp the issue of civil rights. It was only with the eruption of violence in the South in the summer of 1963 that he appeared to cease to temporize, but what is perhaps even more notable is that during that summer, while he was still only the vice-president, none other than Lyndon Johnson was pushing inside the administration for "much more" action by the federal government in the whole area of civil rights. This was not a sudden conversion. As early as 1955 he had, as the majority leader in the Senate, proposed a legislative program that included the abolition of the poll tax, even though Texas still retained it.

There is no way of denying the genuineness with which Johnson's views on civil rights progressed, until it was almost natural for him to proclaim to a joint session of Congress in 1965: "We shall overcome." The evidence is in the record, and it was in the manner in which he spoke of the question in private. He was impassioned to right a wrong; when he talked of the matter, his whole frame moved with a pent-up force, which would not brook denial. He knew the wrong that had been done, he had lived among it, for too long he had tolerated it; and having as a southerner resisted the idea of his own election to the White House, he then as a southerner determined as President to give the last heave that the South needed.

Of course there were electoral considerations. A southern Democrat like Lyndon Johnson, who looked at the Republican inroads into the white urban South in 1952, would naturally look for the voters who could compensate for those losses, so by 1955 he was advocating the federal abolition of poll taxes, even though they were still retained in Texas; and by 1957 he was the main shaper and promoter of a bill to compel the federal protection of voting rights.

But he and the Democratic party knew more of their South than that. They knew their farmers, they knew their rednecks, and for that matter they knew their blacks. Once get them over their hump—the hump John had himself known—and they would still know each other, they would still know their South, and they would still know the Democratic party. And from the other side of that hump, crossed at last, came a man in 1976 who, whenever he may think that he was born again, was in fact born again in 1948 when Hubert Humphrey, a young mayor of Minneapolis in the Far North carried a civil rights amendment through a Democratic National Convention. Jimmy Carter was then twenty-four years old. Humphrey had prepared the way for him.

It does not matter whether we care for the issue of civil rights, or are merely interested in the capacity of the Democratic party to survive, there is a political story in all this that tells us much. Parties must have histories, they must have borne the heat of the day and the fury of the battle, they must have suffered casualties and remember them. Whatever else may be said of the Democratic party in this century, its memories are those of its country, in its trials and suffering.

To hold the blacks and the South, however precariously, after a half century in which it has borne the brunt of a revolution in political and social attitudes, is an accomplishment by any party that needs to be explained, not so much to praise as to try to understand.

Before the election of 1932, the Democratic National Committee turned down a plea from a group of blacks within the party for some mention of race relations in the party's platform; at the election, the party's candidate for vice-president was a white southern racist, John Garner; during the campaign, Roosevelt himself did not mention the subject of race relations. It was only after the election, as he and Jim Farley looked at the results, that they decided that they should seek the black vote in future. This is not cynicism, it is democracy. To have the vote is to be able to force attention to oneself; and if the Republican party after the same election had looked at the returns with an equal interest, it might well have preserved its historic relationship with the northern blacks in the name of Lincoln.

One of the most significant initiatives of Roosevelt's first administration was the introduction of a number of nonpolitical black officials as advisors on race relations. Harold Ickes was persuaded to appoint Clark Foreman, a young white southern liberal, to the new post of Advisor on the Economic Status of Negroes, and Foreman was quickly succeeded by his own black assistant, Robert C.

Weaver, a name that was to stay before the nation for a generation. The actual power of these advisors was not very great; but they were not ineffective as they sought to establish for the blacks at least a legal status of equality, resting their case on the fundamental equalitarian impulse of the New Deal.

It is exactly in this way, if a party is responding to some genuine sense of purpose in itself, that an idea can inform its policy and extend it beyond what originally was intended; and at the same time make the party responsive to the needs of people it needs as voters. This is the legitimate two-way process of democracy.

One of the most important results in the midterm elections of 1934 was the election to Congress from Chicago of Arthur W. Mitchell, the first black Democrat to be returned to the House. Its lesson was clear: the New Deal had split the previously solid Republican black vote in the district, and a Democratic white minority therefore held the electoral balance. That minority worked for Mitchell's return. The next forty years were being prepared. Moreover, the white southern Democrats were unable to retaliate against their party leaders in the North in this period because they were trapped in their own one-party system; and to all of these equations Roosevelt was alert.

In response to the New Deal, the blacks voted heavily for the Democratic party in 1936, and even more heavily in 1940. During the war, the administration gingerly but nonetheless clearly took actions that dramatized its new commitment. It lifted some of the discriminatory restrictions against blacks in the armed services, and it even sent troops to Philadelphia to subdue a violent racist strike of white transit workers who were protesting against the promotion of blacks to be motormen and conductors. In the campaign of 1944, Roosevelt himself advocated a Permanent Fair Employment Practices Commission and the abolition of restrictions on the right of blacks to vote.

The whites in the South were by now growing more restless. Their increasing resistance was symbolized by the Texas Regulars, who were decisively defeated in the Democratic Convention and again in the election when they ran an independent slate against the official party. In March of 1944, the Democratic legislature of South

Carolina had passed a resolution that denounced those who sought "the co-mingling of the races on any basis of equality . . . as being hostile to . . . the preservation of the American Union." But what the farseeing could notice was that this sentiment in 1944 did not save a racist such as "Cotton Ed" Smith from defeat in South Carolina; and it could not prevent the election of liberals such as Claude Pepper in Florida, and Lester Hill in Alabama. As a writer in the *Virginia Quarterly Review* remarked at the time, "The cry of 'Nigger' is losing its magic."

This change of sentiment, however slow, foretold the defeat of the Dixiecrats when they left the party in 1948; and their defeat should in turn have been a warning to the Republicans as they began to build their Southern Strategy on the basis of disaffected white votes. Even in the North, the Republicans did not seem able to take the measure of what was happening. Robert Taft might write to a friend on June 13, 1940: "We have in Ohio and many Northern states an influential colored vote which is really entitled to recognition. The Republican Party came to take this vote for granted, and it was easy for Roosevelt to push it over with the WPA." But exactly three months earlier he had written to another friend: "We ought to get Joe Louis on our side. Your colored friends in Cleveland could perhaps do so." On the one hand, the WPA and the New Deal; in response, the symbolic figure of Joe Louis. There was the difference.

"After the Dixiecrats walked out of the Democratic Convention, there was no question how Negroes would vote" in 1948, said a Harlem editor. "Negroes felt that if they didn't support Truman no other politician would ever defy the Southerners again." Four years later, Adlai Stevenson was able to hold most of the black vote, but in 1956 Eisenhower was able to break into it, although the Republican candidates in other elections were not able to repeat his success. Eisenhower's gains suggested to some that Nixon in 1960 might be able to effect a real breakthrough, but instead Kennedy made substantial gains. "If the Negro voters of America hadn't shifted last Tuesday to John Kennedy," wrote Richard Scammon, the political analyst, after the election, "Vice President Nixon would now be holding press conferences as President-elect."

He called it a "great shift"—it occurred in both the North and the South—and he attributed it in part to the poor performance of the Republican party in office on civil rights, and to the economic recession which, as always, hit the blacks hard and fast. But then he added: "Perhaps most important of all, tying together civil rights *and* economic fears, was the image of candidate Kennedy as a new Roosevelt. For Negro voters Roosevelt remains *the* white man of this century. The dream of a new Roosevelt in the White House may well have been the cause for this massive change of Negro votes"; and that was almost thirty years after Roosevelt had first come to power.

In 1964, as he prepared to push through the greatest measures of civil rights and voting rights in this century, Lyndon Johnson carried the black vote, North and South, with the kind of overwhelming majority that one usually associates with the window-dressing elections in a dictatorship; and with the exception of the election of 1972, in which George McGovern demonstrated his ability to throw away huge blocs of votes he needed and could have had, the story has remained much the same ever since, until a white southerner in 1976 could rely on the black vote, North and South, as on no other bloc.

Simply as a story, even without a moral, it is amazing. It is hard to think of any other party in any of the Western democracies that has so instinctively and then so resolutely been ready to identify itself with a subject minority in the nation, as it came forward to make its claim on society, and whose votes it needed. The loyalty of the black vote—unless it is unduly provoked as in 1972—is born of trust; and it must be recognized that the basis of that trust is to be found, not in attitudes to color and race but in attitudes to poverty and class.

Samuel Lubell noticed this as far back as 1948. "Dewey's record in behalf of the Negro surpassed that of any previous New York governor," he said. "But, if Dewey could appeal to the Negro's race consciousness, he could not surmount the Negro's consciousness of being part of the lower economic class"; and he added: "The basic reason why the Republicans have been unable to recapture the Negro vote lies in their inability to identify themselves with the climbing aspirations of the black masses," as they had also been unable to identify themselves with the urban masses of other ethnic groups.

The story may be amazing even without a moral, but the moral is clear. It is an economic perception of society, an awareness of the class differences that exist in a misnamed condition of affluence, which keeps the Democratic party on course. This is its truth, that there are still classes in America, that there are still the unaffluent and that it alone is willing to represent them; and without this truth it loses its purpose, its direction; its imagination; even its soul. It also loses its votes. It cannot win without a substantial turnout of lower-income voters, whatever class label one may attach to them. In 1968, when the Democratic party was in such disarray, 32 percent of the northern working class voted for Humphrey, 26 percent for Nixon, and 9 percent for Wallace, but what mattered even more was that 31 percent of them, a much higher proportion than usual, simply did not go to the polls.

Among the working class were and are, North and South, the blacks and other nonwhites. The programs of the New Deal were not aimed primarily at them: Their purpose was to "free from fear" in their day-to-day lives the main body of white Americans, and the nonwhites benefited, with the exception of a few measures, only incidentally and marginally. But the Great Society was specifically addressed to "that one-fifth" of the population, as Lyndon Johnson put it, who could not afford even the basic wants of life, and that one-fifth included a large proportion of the nonwhite population. It was to these that Lyndon Johnson sought to bring "equality as a fact, and equality as a result."

The faults of the Great Society programs were so obvious that its genuine achievements have in recent years tended to be overlooked. But the fact is that, as three careful observers have put it, it was government action in the 1960s, under two Democratic administrations, that "clearly served as the primary catalyst and engine for change," in the situation of the nonwhites. The gains made were needed and substantial, and lasting in their effect, even though they were then to be eroded during the Republican administrations that followed. The ratio of nonwhite to white median family income, which had been stable between 1950 and 1965, rose from 55 percent to 64 percent in the next five years, but then fell back to 62 percent in the first half of the 1970s. The number of poor blacks fell from 9.9 million to 7.1 million in the 1960s, but then increased again to 7.5 million by 1974. The examples could be multiplied.

Lyndon Johnson and the Great Society were not following the literate liberals in perceiving the primary concern of politics to be "the nature of our culture"; they did not think with Arthur Schlesinger that the need for "quantitative liberalism," concerned with jobs and wages, housing and welfare, had been replaced by a need for "qualitative liberalism," concerned with the quality of life for the affluent. In the 1960s the Democratic party seemed to have returned, after the Stevenson years, to its basic concern in this century: to improve the conditions and opportunities of the underprivileged and the dispossessed. And this was again the basic appeal of Jimmy Carter in 1976, of which he was then persistently reminded when he took office.

This was as true in the South in 1976 as in the North. That revealing question: "The blacks, the farmers, and the rednecks. Who else is there?" was a remark about poverty in the South, made by a man who knew the South. When "Cotton Ed" Smith raised the cry of "Nigger" in 1944, he also said that workers in South Carolina, white as well as black, could live on fifty cents a day. The workers of South Carolina did not believe him, and turned him out. The class divisions in American society and therefore in its politics may have been blurred by a greater national prosperity, and by the growth of the suburbs, but they have not been abolished; and the Democratic party and its leaders need not to forget this.

The War Party and
Its Dilemma

THROUGHOUT 1968 IT WAS hard to understand why, because of his opposition to American intervention in Vietnam, Eugene McCarthy was perceived by so many as a liberal, and even as a radical. No more upstanding conservative had been a Democratic candidate for the presidential nomination since Adlai Stevenson. In his general attitudes to what he perceived to be the proper business of government he was not far removed from Calvin Coolidge.

When he said after his victory in the Oregon primary that if he won the election he would tear down the railings that surround the White House, many of his followers took it as a wonderful signal of how accessible to the people he would make the presidency. But of course what he really meant was that he would make the presidency so unimportant that no one would ever think of going to the White House at all, unless perhaps for poetry readings. In 1973, he was the moderator of a seminar at the New School in New York on "The Crisis of the Presidency," which was rather like putting a teetotaler in charge of a wine-tasting; and in an after-dinner speech he in effect argued for the transformation of the president into a prime minister. It was not surprising. Whatever the value of his initial protest in 1968, he was in fact running for the wrong office in the wrong country.

Adlai Stevenson was a convinced opponent of big government, and so was McCarthy, who had put Stevenson's name in nomination at the Democratic Convention in 1960, against that of Kennedy. His speech on that occasion was magnificent and, rather like Roosevelt when he nominated Al Smith in 1928, McCarthy seemed to be picking the mantle off the shoulders of the man he was championing. There was the same elegant articulacy in him as in Stevenson, and to many of the literate liberals, as well as to a new generation of the children of the affluent on the college campuses, that articulacy was as seductive as before. But what must interest us most is that both were conservatives.

His own memoir of the campaign in 1968—which is strangely called *The Year of the People,* a year in which the people stayed at home in large numbers on election day, and Richard Nixon was consequently returned to the White House—is almost a primer of conservatism, not least in its tone of voice. When he calls for "a revived sense of profession and vocation in modern society," he is in fact repeating one of the classic conservative appeals against contemporary democracy. When he applauds the fact that in Minnesota there had never for any length of time been "uneducated minorities who could be controlled or manipulated by party leaders," one hears not only a disdain for the bosses and their machines, but a sniff at the "uneducated minorities" themselves. When in one of his many acerbic and often telling observations about the Kennedys he says that Robert Kennedy had "set up twenty-six different committees to deal with different kinds of Americans," and added that "I did not know there were that many," the voice is superior, and it is conservative; and it is in this context that one must judge what he calls "my effort to depersonalize the Presidency," by which he usually seems to mean an operation as radical as a change of sex. Yet there were liberals who, because of his stand on one issue, saw him as a hero of a "new politics."

In a way he did represent the new politics of the affluent and their children; and he was clearly enough a WASP to do well in places like New Hampshire, where the uneducated minorities are less numerous than other animals. The much-vaunted "Children's Crusade" was largely a protest by prosperous college students against a war they did not want to fight. They may have been right not to want to fight in that war, but that does not alter the fact that as soon as the draft was abolished the antiwar movement on the campuses collapsed; and they turned to consider "The nature of the culture" the exquisiteness of their sensibilities.

By 1976 even those who had previously supported him, and were still grateful for his stand eight years before, recognized him as a spoiler. The smallness of spirit his associates had often detected in him was now seen as a smallness in public spirit as well. Many of the major figures in his campaign in 1968 contributed to an advertisement in 1976 which proclaimed: "McCARTHY SAYS HE DOESN'T CARE IF HIS VOTES HELP REELECT FORD—WE DO." It could hardly have been put plainer: on the one hand, a generous concern for the public welfare; on the other, a small-spirited desire for personal revenge. It is more than possible that McCarthy could have helped Hubert Humphrey to win in 1968, and so prevent the election of Nixon, but he could not bring himself to do it. After all, if the presidency matters so little, if it should be so depersonalized, what difference does it make who is elected from which party to fill it?

Hubert Humphrey has had the opportunity to know well the man who was once his fellow senator from Minnesota, and his observations are biting. McCarthy is "a clever politician, cleverer for denying it," he says. "He often ridiculed some of the things I did. But he does that to most people. Basically, Gene disdains whatever peer group he is in. If he was teaching college students, he found most of his colleagues dull. When he was in the House, he grew tired of congressmen. In the Senate, he found few senators or senatorial duties that interested him." When Humphrey asked him about his candidacy, McCarthy said in effect: "Well, I don't have any feeling that I can win, but I don't like the Senate. I've lost interest in it."

None of this is intended to question the fact that McCarthy, as he put it, "felt very strongly about the war" by 1968, although he had not until then been one of the leading "doves" in the Senate, and had supported the Gulf of Tonkin resolution, and voted for appropriations for the American intervention. We are concerned here merely about his seriousness as a politician. He did not withhold his support from Humphrey on principle; he eventually gave an endorsement, but it was "less than enthusiastic," as Humphrey puts it; and when one considers what happened under Nixon, McCarthy's responsibility for the catastrophe seems considerable.

Here is exactly the point at which political character (or the lack of it) and political principle (or the lack of it) are joined, and at which adherence to party, which does not mean an unquestioning obedience to it, is one of the ways in which political character may be measured. It is hard to detect an underlying thread of political principle in the career of Eugene McCarthy, and he is an outstanding example of the kind of man whose political character might have been made stronger if the whims of his personal motives had been been regulated by disciplined association the steadiness of a party's beliefs.

Perhaps the Democratic party needed his conservative voice in 1968 more than even he understood, for it is no surprise that the natural opposition to the American intervention in Vietnam should have been most acidly expressed by conservatives like himself and William Fulbright, another elegantly articulate man who attracted the literate liberals. A conservative such as Fulbright, who does not believe that the federal government should do much about anything—especially about the blacks in Arkansas—is likely to be opposed to such an effort to the federal government as it made in Southeast Asia; and Robert Taft might well have been Fulbright's most certain ally.

When Lyndon Johnson began talking of building the Great Society, not only in America, but in Southeast Asia as well—and there was a kind of lunacy in the proposal —one can well understand the horror with which men such as McCarthy and Fulbright raised their hands in pious affront: "Enough! . . . Enough!" And of course it was with less pious affront that a fiscal conservative such as Wilbur Mills, as chairman of the House Ways and Means Committee, immediately began to pin down Johnson by the short hairs, refusing him both guns and butter, before the more popular opposition to the war had really detonated.

Taft would have been with them, in the same spirit as when he said of Roosevelt in 1939 that "no one has ever suggested before that a single nation should range over the world like a knight errant"; and of the Atlantic Charter that it was "a declaration that the United States and England should run the world"; and not least when he immediately opposed the Truman Doctrine. Taft was in many ways the forerunner not of a conservative Republican such as Goldwater but a conservative Democrat such as Fulbright.

We are here at a crucial point; one might almost say that we have come to the crunch. The Democratic party in this century has been a missionary party, at home and abroad. It was perhaps inevitable in the historical context that it should be. Some party had to take the responsibility—make the errors, and bear the wounds—for adapting the conduct of the United States in the world to the fact that the conditions of its previous isolation had ended, and to the reality of the fact that it had become the most powerful nation in the world, and therefore could not avoid the exercise of its huge power. As the normal governing party in this century, the Democrats have had to undertake that task.

That is the truth, as it is also the honor, in Robert Dole's description of the First World War, and then the Second World War, and then the Korean War, as "Democrat wars." He was making a sleazy point, and he was making it sleazily; but the fact is that it is the Democratic party in this century that has borne on its own body the injuries of the nation, as it has met the responsibilities of its power.

In 1940, under severe pressure from his advisors, Franklin Roosevelt gave his pledge that under his administration no American boy would die on foreign soil. When he first uttered these words, from the back of a train, he returned to his compartment, according to the account of Harry Hopkins, and was sick. He had told what he knew to be a lie; and what is more, any American at the time who was capable of thinking straight must have known that he was telling a lie. But if he believed that he was the right man, and that the Democrats were the right party, to take the country into a necessary war, and to fight the

war, should it come, energetically and with conviction, then the lie had to be told, even if it made him sick. The moral imperatives of power are not those of personal life.

But an acceptance of the unavoidable responsibilities of the exercise of great power is different from a missionary impulse. That impulse was strong in Woodrow Wilson. As his biographer, John A. Garraty, says, his foreign policy was "moralistic, philanthropic, evangelical, and curiously ethnocentric and unrealistic." It was Lodge and not Wilson who argued that American intervention in Mexico should be on "the true and international ground" of the protection of American life and property, and Wilson who made it seem like a quixotic adventure in defense of democracy and high ideals. In January 1918, when Wilson determined to issue his Fourteen Points, he called Edward M. House, the American ambassador in London, to the White House. "Saturday was a remarkable day," House wrote in his diary. "We actually got down to work at half-past ten and finished remaking the map of the world, as we would have it, at half-past twelve o'clock."

"As we would have it": There was the missionary impulse in a nutshell. Isolationism was in part a resistance to this impulse, and it was expressed most strongly by conservatives. Arthur Vandenberg said of the lend-lease provisions in 1940 that they "needlessly make President Roosevelt the Ace Power Politician of The World," and "turn The White House into G.H.Q. for all the wars in all the world." In the colossal American effort in the Second World War, in the Marshall Plan, in the Truman Doctrine, in the Korean War, in the intervention in Vietnam, the missionary impulse was always a strong factor. Against this impulse, it was characteristic of a conservative such as Taft that he should say in 1943: "I do not believe that any war can be justified as a crusade. . . . [A] crusade by its very nature is an aggressive act." But it was Eisenhower who adopted the cross of the Crusaders as the insignia of his armies, and who called his memoirs of the war *Crusade in Europe*. Changed times alter perspectives.

But it is here that we must be careful if we are to understand the dilemma of the Democrats, their impulse to be missionary, and the resistance of conservatives to that impulse. The problem is not as easy as revisionist historians would have us believe.

Henry Wallace may be remembered best now as the opponent of the cold war and of American resistance to Russian expansionism. But in his diary for November 2, 1942, he wrote that he would discuss with Roosevelt "the need for taking the offensive with regard to an international New Deal"; and also in his diary, a few months before, agreeing with Winthrop Aldrich that "it would be necessary for the United States to furnish worldwide leadership" after the war, he added: "The loan without the lender is bare."

What is interesting about these statements is that, especially in the proposal for "an international New Deal," they reflect the same missionary impulse of Lyndon Johnson in his proposal to create a Great Society in Southeast Asia. If this were not a dilemma for the Democrats, it would not be interesting. If the dilemma were not honorable, the Democratic party would not have emerged with so much honor from its fearful history in this century.

One may put it the other way round. On the first full day that he was president, Lyndon Johnson met Walter Heller, the chairman of the Council of Economic Advisers, at 7:40 P.M. "Heller had come to ask me an urgent question: Did I want the Council of Economic Advisers to develop a program to attack poverty." Johnson tells us that "I swung round my chair and looked out of the window. Lights were burning in the West Wing of the White House, across Executive Avenue, in the offices of grief-stricken men." He "turned back and looked into Heller's eyes," a man who was submerging his grief in his "work that looked toward the future." Johnson's reply was not seriously in doubt.

A month later, during the Christmas holidays, the poverty program was worked out at the LBJ Ranch, and "the title War on Poverty was decided on during those days. It had its disadvantages. . . . But I wanted to rally the nation, to sound a call to arms." In his first State of the Union message, he announced that his administration was declaring "unconditional war on poverty in America"; and in another message to Congress in March 1964, he described poverty as a "domestic enemy."

There was the language of war—of unconditional war, no less—brought home to excite a missionary impulse against a "domestic enemy"; and there is no point in re-

fusing to recognize that, in an activist party, there is a very difficult line to be drawn between a mission to do good at home and a mission to do good abroad.

In his personal decision—against which he was strongly advised—to throw all his weight behind the civil rights bill in 1964, Lyndon Johnson recalled the remark of John Garner, "a great legislative tactician, as well as a good poker player," that "there comes a time in every leader's career when he has to put in all his stack. I decided to shove in all my stack on this vital measure." But then he decided to throw in all his stack also, in order to save democracy in an Asian country that had never known democracy, and to create a Great Society where it could not be rationally attempted.

The dilemma is one the Democratic party has not yet resolved. How can the impulse to do good at home, without which it would not be the Democratic party, not excite a similar impulse to do good abroad. A Democratic party which had had Eugene McCarthy as president in 1964, and William Fulbright as majority leader of the Senate, would not have passed the civil rights bill, or even attempted to pass a majority of the measures of the Great Society.

Moreover, the dilemma was exposed again in the election campaign in 1976. The shock that ran through most people when Jimmy Carter said in one of the presidential debates that he would not send American troops to Yugoslavia in the event of a Russian invasion was not only at the obvious imprudence of handing over one's own revolver to an armed burglar; there was also the shock that the spokesman of the Democratic party should say such a thing.

For the Democratic party has in this century been the war party because the nation has in this troubled century had to be a warring nation. There has been no escape for either. The party and the nation had to go to war in 1917; they had to go to war in 1941; they had in the historical context to go to war in Korea; and, again in the historical context, the original commitment to Vietnam was at the time questioned by very few people, either in America or in the rest of the free world. That the Democratic party has undertaken this responsibility, that it has borne the sufferings of the nation, carried its wounds as its own, been one of the casualties more than once, is a mark of honor, and it is one reason it seems to belong to its own times as the Republicans do not; because it has borne the sufferings also of the immigrants, it has borne the wounds also of the Depression, and it has for a time been a casualty also of the struggle for civil rights for the uneducated minorities.

It has been ready to fight, at home and abroad, and that is not to be disregarded; because the nation itself has had to fight, at home and abroad, in a tumultuous century. But there has been a flaw, against which even the misdirected resistance of the conservatives has warned; and the source of that flaw is apparent. As we turn to examine it, one may say that the eradication of that flaw, without reaching to the conservative solution, ought to be the main task to which Jimmy Carter addresses himself.

"Big Government" and the "Imperial Presidency"

THERE IS SOMETHING MORE THAN a little deceitful, and certainly a lot that is absurd, in a presidential candidate who is trying to get to Washington by saying that he is running "against Washington," and who hopes to be elected to the most powerful office in the world by proclaiming that he is against big government. A saloon-keeper might as well justify his application for a license by saying that he is a member of the Temperance Reform League. It is as if Julius Caesar, after reading the omens from the disemboweled entrails of a goose, had exhorted his troops to cross the Rubicon by saying that their purpose was to seize Rome and make it again a village.

If this is true of any presidential candidate, it is especially true of a Democratic candidate. The American people have not known the Democratic party in power for so much of the past half century to imagine that by voting for it, they are voting for someone who will not use the powers of the federal government. If they want a do-little administration, they know where to look; and however bewildered they may have been by the character of Jimmy Carter in 1976, and by the representations of it in

213

the press, even the most obtuse of them must have recognized that here was a man, bent on power, who would exercise the federal authority to the full.

"Big government" is really a misnomer. The bigness of government is no guarantee of its strength or activity or effectiveness; in fact, mere bigness in itself can be the enemy of each of these. But popular phrases are not to be lightly rejected. Anyone in the twentieth century may say that he is in favor of government that is strong and active and effective. The phrase *"big government"* is needed to emphasize a difference that is not otherwise easily stated.

Few men helped to create the atmosphere in which the Democratic party in the 1930s established its dominance more than the philosopher John Dewey. In 1935, he looked back to the liberal philosophers at the end of the nineteenth century who had tried to rescue liberalism from an out-of-date laissez-faire and bring it into harmony with the new collectivist spirit of the age. "These new liberals fostered the idea," he said, "that the state has the responsibility for creating institutions under which individuals can effectively realize the potentialities that are theirs." They were "committed to the principle that organized society must use its powers to establish the conditions under which the mass of individuals can possess actual as distinct from merely legal liberty." There was the ambition of the New Deal in two sentences.

Organized society with the state as its most effective instrument: that is why it is worth retaining the popular talk of big government. Organized society in this century means big society; it means big business and big labor, big technology and big institutions; and against the pressure of all these other "bignesses" it is "big government," alone elected by the whole people and accountable to them, that must be the main defender.

Such has been the profoundest belief of the Democratic party in this century. "The 'New Freedom'" of Woodrow Wilson, one historian has said, "meant exactly what it said—the restoration of individual competition." This was in direct opposition to the "New Nationalism" of Theodore Roosevelt, which sought to meet the same problems not by the competition of business but by the regulation of it. But when Wilson tried to secure the passage of his tariff bill in 1913, which sought to compel the first significant reduction in duties since the Civil War, he was enraged by the lobbyists of big business. "Washington has seldom seen so numerous, so industrious, or so insidious a lobby," he declared. "It is of serious interest to this country that the people of this country should have no lobby . . . while great bodies of astute men seek to create an artificial opinion . . . for their private profit." At the same time, he followed the progressives in his party who refused to let the national currency remain in the private control of the bankers, and created the Federal Reserve Board.

The "New Freedom" he had advocated was turning perceptibly into the "New Nationalism" of his most formidable opponent; and in that change there lies much of the history of the two parties as they have developed in this century.

If the big private institutions of modern society have their lobbies, then the people should have their lobby in big government: This was one of the themes of the New Deal, and it was especially a repeated theme of Harry Truman's, who believed that without the federal government the people would be unrepresented in Washington. It was in turn this attitude that he urged on Lyndon Johnson.

In spite of all the talk of the feeling "against Washington" that is supposed to exist in the country, it is hard to see any way in which the Democratic party, without destroying itself, can reverse this now traditional belief. "It is a little as if at last America had marched on Washington," wrote Anne O'Hare McCormick at the beginning of the New Deal. "The United States has been brought to Washington, more dependent on government than it has ever been in history, and demanding omnipotent gestures from government, as many as are necessary to get the machine in motion." That may not be quite the mood of the country now, but it is equally clear that the country is not by any means marching away from Washington, and neither can the Democrats march away from it when they in fact occupy it, almost willy-nilly.

The enjoyment of the Democratic party in politics is in part a reflection of its belief in government. "Democrats seem to love government, while, I suspect, high-level Republicans too often really do not," says Hubert Humphrey.

"For too many of them, service in Washington is nothing more than a break between two jobs in private industry, or banking or law, and the art of government is itself less appealing, less exciting than it is to Democrats."

The appeal of politics to the Democrat lies in the opportunity to do things. He does not pray for rain, as we have seen, he takes measures to meet the drought. The Cabinet under Eisenhower began with prayer; a Democratic Cabinet does not pray, because it is convinced that it can take events into its own hands. The Republicans would have criticized the Lord for hastening to complete the world in six days; the Democrats would have criticized him for taking so long, appointed itself his earthly viceroy, and done the thing by executive order, in a day or two.

There can be dangers in this. Necessary action may be replaced by unnecessary activity. Too much government can defeat itself, and be not strong but weak. The wrong climate may be too easily created, and the problems of peace tackled as if they are the same as the problems of war, as in the "call to arms" in the War on Poverty. Raymond Moley was already a disgruntled renegade from the New Deal when he wrote of its First Hundred Days that "Official Washington was in the grip of a war psychology as surely as it had been in 1917"; but even someone who recognizes the need for such an atmosphere at that time can also think that there was something in the psychology that ought not to be taken as a precedent.

The entire administration of John Kennedy was in "the grip of a war psychology." The men who put such faith in guerrilla warfare abroad resorted with the same eagerness to a form of guerrilla government at home. Just as it is necessary to bypass many of the normal procedures of government in war, so Kennedy and his administration tried to bypass many of its normal procedures in peace. But to criticize such methods is not to criticize strong and active government as such. On the contrary, it helps to direct our attention to the way in which Democrats might escape from their dilemma, by making a distinction between big government in itself and the claims of an overweening and "imperial presidency."

One of the reasons the political character of their presidential candidates is of so much concern to the Democrats and to the people in general is that they both expect a Democratic president to be strong and active, and to use his executive power to the full. The image of Roosevelt is still strong in Democratic minds and in the folk memory of the country: *That* is what a Democratic president should and will be like, is the popular conception.

Much is written today about the exaltation of the imperial presidency under Roosevelt, and it was criticized at the time by the Republicans. Even before America had entered the war in 1941, Vandenberg wrote in his journal that "the limitations on 'free speech' are getting constantly more apparent—and I suppose it won't be long before *lèse majesté* is an *American* crime." Moreover, the presidency seemed to be being exalted at the expense of the legislature, in prestige as well as in power. Vandenberg complained in September 1941 to Lord Beaverbrook that he "had not been invited to the executive office in eight years," and he added: "I do not care to record Beaverbrook's responsive comment. But it would burn a hole in this paper." He like Taft spoke despondently of "the ultimate end of our democracy."

Neither were the Republicans alone. Come from the cornbrake of Louisiana, with "great intellectual capacity," and "a tremendous emotional and psychological drive," as a journalist put it at the time, with "a sudden, compelling, dramatic presence—in white shoes, a cream-colored suit, and an orange tie," as Humphrey remembers him, Huey Long thundered to the Senate on April 5, 1935: "You aren't even trying to legislate. You've turned your powers and duties over to [the New Dealers]. The laws they've passed in the privacy of their offices would fill volumes." But his fellow Democrats in Congress did not agree with him.

The reasons for elevating the presidency over not only the legislature but the rest of the executive are many and complex. Some lie in the American form of government, which Macaulay described to an American friend as "all sail, and no anchor." Others lie in the unavoidable nature of modern government, and in the vastness of the power and wealth which the United States has at its command. But there is also a particular reason why the Democratic party is tempted to exalt it.

Woodrow Wilson was persuaded that he was the unchallengeable voice of the people—he seemed to translate *"Vox populi, vox dei"* as "I am the voice of the people, therefore I am god"—and the main instrument of power on which he relied was an appeal to the public opinion of which he believed he was the master. "I kept the pressure of opinion constantly on the legislature," he said when he was governor of New Jersey. Since he believed that "no one but the President seems to be expected . . . to look out for the general interest of the country," he interpreted all his own actions as a realization of the people's will. When he read of resistance in the Senate to the League of Nations, he commented: "Those Senators do not know what the people are thinking. They are as far from the people, the great mass of people, as I am from Mars." And something of this accent has continued in Democratic presidents ever since.

Roosevelt often sought to govern over the heads of Congress by direct appeals to the people in his fireside chats. Truman again and again appealed to the popular mind, as in his proposal to draft strikers which he made in a broadcast address even when the strike at issue had that afternoon been settled. Kennedy used to appear before the people on television like a Byzantine emperor, sheathed in gold, suspended between earth and heaven.

And of course as great a populist as Johnson expressed this habit vividly. "Every President has to establish with the various sections of the country what I call 'the right to govern.' Just being elected does not guarantee that right. . . . Every President has to develop a moral underpinning to his power, or he soon discovers that he has no power at all." That moral underpinning is to be found mainly in a direct relationship between the president and the people, and the justification is ready. As Truman had said to Johnson on his elevation to the presidency, "the duty of the President was to lead and champion the people's causes." In short, the president is the voice of the people.

Much of the damage that the Democratic party has done to itself and to the country in this century, among all the good, has been caused, not by its belief in big government as such, but by its exaggerated and false belief in what at times seems to be an almost mystical relationship between the president and the people. The most unlimited expression of this relationship followed what was in effect the coronation of John Kennedy, and for almost three years he and his family and his court were elevated to be not only the leaders of a party the governors of a nation, but the rulers of its culture, the arbiters of its taste; virtually the priests of its society. John Kennedy had in fact marched on Washington much as an upstart general used to march on Rome and claim the emperor's wreath; and he governed as an emperor.

Yet the Democratic party should know better than any other that this is not how a democracy is best governed, nor how it may best earn the sustained trust of the people. The lesson of the history of the Democratic party in this century is that politics is a multifarious activity: boisterous and untidy, a game to be played as much for its own sake, because the purpose of the game is never clear from day to day, and played to the hilt, with lust and gusto.

That was the lesson which it learned from the streets of the cities, from the immigrants whom it sheltered and befriended and welcomed, from the bosses and their lieutenants, from the ward heelers and the precinct captains, from the great congressional leaders in mid century; and above all it was the lesson that it should have learned from Franklin Roosevelt, who may have elevated the presidency, especially during the conditions of a world war, but who never forget that politics is a rough-and-tumble, in which the moment when "push comes to shove" is always likely to have to be met when it is least expected and least welcome. This is not the politics of monarchs or emperors.

The new president does not only need a Congress that is alert and abrasive. He needs also, and perhaps even more, a party that does not stand in awe of him, that will be rough with him, will instruct him, will remind him that great parties are repositories of popular wisdom more reliable than his own divinations of the popular mind. But to be such a party, such a prod to the president when necessary, and when necessary such a check on him, the Democrats must as a party believe in their own purpose, formed before he was elected, and to survive after he has left. But it is this that they now lack.

A Wee Bit to Left
of Center

"MR. ROOSEVELT IS NOW, as always, just a wee bit to left of center," as I. F. Stone wrote in 1944, when Roosevelt made his fourth appeal to the electors. Not everyone agreed with Stone. At about the same time, Marriner Eccles, the chairman of the Federal Reserve Board, said that Roosevelt "is not a liberal any more," and that "he does a lot of funny political things." Eliot Janeway, the economic journalist, remarked that "the Tories will win in 1944" and, when asked what he meant by that, he answered: "Oh, Roosevelt and the gang around him will get back in power again." Yet "a wee bit to left of center" was in fact where Roosevelt stood, as he even advocated the establishment of a permanent Fair Employment Practices Commission.

What is more, it is a little to the left of center where the Democratic party has usually found itself standing in this century, and where it has always found itself pushed in order to win. When Jimmy Carter chose Walter Mondale as his vice-presidential candidate, he was acting wholly within the tradition of the party in this century. He might say that he was a fiscal conservative, and in fact be one;

but in the election as distinct from the primaries he took his campaign perceptibly to the left of center. He made the party recognizably the beast with which the people have for long been familiar.

More than sixty years earlier, when he was running to be governor of New Jersey, Woodrow Wilson found it necessary to move from the right to the left of center. By the end of his campaign, this naturally conservative man was proclaiming, "I am and always have been an insurgent," which no one would have known from his past; and it was in this mood that he said, "I regard myself as pledged to the regeneration of the Democratic Party," and this meant that it would be regenerated as a progressive force. Convictions that he had long held were abandoned "in the course of a couple of speeches," as promise of reform was added to promise, to attract the liberals and the progressives.

While he was governor, these promises were not forgotten. He drove through the state legislature an impressive program of new laws, both of political reform and social improvement. He had become "a militant liberal almost overnight," as one of his biographers puts it, and in this he was responding to a national mood, in particular to the social unrest that had agitated the country for two decades. He became a politician of his time, and as such he won and governed.

We may watch him do much the same in 1916, when he was seeking reelection to the presidency, without the advantage, which he had enjoyed in 1912, of facing a divided Republican party. In nine months in 1916, as the election drew near, he and the Democratic party "enacted almost every important plank in the Progressive platform of 1912." In quick succession he signed a Farm Loan Act, which created federal land banks to sustain a system of adequate rural credit, a federal child labor law, and the Adamson Act, which established an eight-hour day for railroad workers: all measures he had previously condemned. His earlier strict constitutionalism and laissez-faire economics had given way before what he perceived to be the national mood and the demands of the electoral situation.

He only just won—there were days of anguish before

the final results brought the reassurance that he had been reelected—but what is certain is that he would not have won if he had not moved again sufficiently to the left of center to find the votes that he needed, and taken the Democratic party with him. The party of the next sixty years was at last being defined after its long years in opposition: the very party onto whose shoulders Carter could climb in 1976.

Against these victories of Wilson may be set the failure of the Democratic party in 1920, and his own responsibility for that failure, even though he was not the candidate. The main cause of the defeat was his own disastrous inability and that of his administration to cope effectively with domestic policy in the aftermath of the First World War. The economy was left to drift, social unrest was greater even than before, big business and the unions were engaged in what business at least intended to be a struggle to the death, and the repression of elementary civil liberties was widespread. Obsessed with his plans for remaking the world, he ignored the plight of the country and millions of its people at home; and in doing so, he destroyed the very moral authority which he needed if he was to carry his scheme for a League of Nations. When he took his crusade to the people, appealing to them over the heads of the Senate, it was to a people whose trust he had forfeited, mainly as a result of his neglect of their most immediate and day-to-day needs. He had eroded his own power.

During the 1920s the Democratic party did not recover its reformist impulse. It was disunited and purposeless, and the home only of factions. Indeed, the representative figure of the Democratic party in that decade might be said to be the man who died suddenly (but hardly before it was time for the nation's good) in the middle of it. Wilson once said to a friend that William Jennings Bryan lacked a "mental rudder." Al Smith described him as an opportunist: "Bryan did the thing that helped Bryan." In an obituary notice of unforgiving harshness, Walter Lippmann refused to "construct a eulogy" for this "natural-born maker and leader of factions."

"As a Democrat he spent his chief energies quarreling with Democrats, and as a Christian he ended his life quarreling angrily with other Christians" was Lippmann's summary; and it was not until he had died, and not until the Democratic party then turned, with the nomination of Smith, to gather the votes of the disregarded immigrants in the cities to itself, that it began to move back to its natural stance in this century, somewhat to the left of center.

By 1934 Harold Ickes was writing in his diary that the New Deal was dead; a year later even he could see that, if it had been dead, it was very much alive again. Whether or not there was a "Second New Deal"—a phrase to juggle with, rather than to ponder over—there can be no doubt that in 1935, as he prepared to make his first appeal for reelection, Franklin Roosevelt began to emphasize his programs for reform, and not merely those for recovery: In order to meet the people, he moved emphatically to the left of center, and there he found them. Although he later became more and more immersed in foreign affairs, and although he himself proclaimed the passing of "Dr. New Deal," he could be observed at each of the two succeeding elections moving a little to the left in order to make his appeal.

Bernard De Voto might speak for many liberals in 1944 when he said that Roosevelt's administration had by then become "tired, cynical, shifty, strained by its inner contradictions, grown as doubtful of its original ends as it is confused about its means," which was a fairly sweeping indictment of a government that was leading a worldwide alliance in a major war; but the fact of the matter is that even then Roosevelt was still willing to pursue his "original ends," not least by carrying his own overt advocacy of civil rights for the blacks much farther than he had done before.

He was always looking for the votes he and his party needed, and he always found them by moving at least a little to the left. "I have always believed, and I have frequently stated," he himself wrote in the introduction to volume 7 of his public papers, "that my own party can succeed at the polls only so long as it continues to be the party of militant liberalism." He was defending his intervention in the primary campaigns of 1938 to secure the nomination of liberal or progressive candidates—what

was "slurringly referred to," as he put it, as a "purge"—
and he left no doubt what he meant by liberalism. "The
liberal party"—by which in the twentieth century he
meant the Democratic party—"insists that the government
has the definite duty to use all its power and resources
to meet new social problems with new social controls."
Whether one likes it or not, this was his legacy, and the
Democratic party has not yet found an alternative.

The legacy at first had an inheritor. As the 1948 election drew near, Harry Truman shifted his stance as
perceptibly to the left of center as Roosevelt had ever
done; and again the result was victory, and again it must
be doubted if he could have won if he had not decided to
move to the left, to obey the prescription of Roosevelt,
that only as a party of militant liberalism can the Democratic party hope to succeed at the polls.

But almost thirty years later, even the apparent
standard-bearer of the liberals in 1976, Morris Udall, was
asking that he should not be labeled a liberal. Yet it was
by the nomination of a liberal to run with him, and by
the all but unqualified adoption of a liberal rhetoric, that
Carter at last held together the fundamental support that
he needed. There is a paradox here and if the Democrats
are, not only to win elections, but to govern well, it needs
to be resolved. A party cannot at once be liberal and be
afraid to be known and to know itself as liberal. It cannot
afford to submit to a conservative seduction of its spirit.

On September 23, 1953, John Kenneth Galbraith wrote
to Adlai Stevenson, saying that the Democratic party had
been trading for too long on the ideas and ideals of the
New Deal, adding that this "capital is running thin." But
it is too easy to say that it was then or now running thin,
when the Democratic party is forced again and again to
return to it, and when it is very difficult to see how the
Democrats can dispense with the fundamental principles
that Roosevelt laid down for its guidance in 1938.

We should follow his words with care. "The system of
party responsibility in America requires that one of its
parties be the liberal party and the other the conservative
party." *Is that any less true now than in 1938?*

"The clear and undisputed fact is that in these later

years, at least since 1932, the Democratic Party has been the liberal party, and the Republican Party has been the conservative party." *Is that any less true now than in 1938?*

"The liberal group has always believed that control by a few—political control or economic control—if exercised for a long period of time, would be destructive of sound representative democracy." *Is that any less true now than in 1938?*

"The liberal party is a party which believes that, as new conditions and problems arise beyond the power of men and women to meet as individuals, it becomes the duty of the government itself to find new remedies with which to meet them." *Is that any less true now than in 1938?*

"The conservative party believes that there is no necessity for the government to step in, even when new conditions and new problems arise. It believes that, in the long run, individual initiative and private philanthropy can take care of all situations." *Is that any less true now than in 1938?*

"The conservative generally believes that all remedies proposed by the government are usually unnecessary, and that perfection can be obtained more readily and more quickly through private initiative. *Is that any less true now than in 1938?*

He went on to criticize not the liberal who is a liberal or the conservative who is a conservative but those who "pretend to be one thing but who act the other," and he was particularly critical of the liberal who "says, 'Yes' —that he is in favor of the end; *but* he objects to the means—at the same time offering no alternative method, and seldom, if ever, raising a finger of his own to try to obtain the ultimate objective. I have frequently referred to this type of individual as a 'yes, but—' fellow."

There is more in these simple—although also astute—politician's words, addressed to the moment, than in many volumes of political analysis. This is still—in American terms—what a liberal is and—in American terms—it is still what a conservative is. It is still the Democratic party that exists to represent the other. This was still what was the issue in the election in 1936.

To say that this "capital is running thin" for liberal or conservative, for Democrat or Republican, is to deny the primary issue of this century, and what is perceived by the electors to be the primary issue: the extent to which modern technological society, with its inevitable concentrations of power, needs and ought to be brought under the governance of democratic political institutions that are strong and active and efficient. There is no way in which the government of such a society is going to be weak and inactive. The issue is whether it will be strong government for the rich and the few, or strong government for the unrich and the many. For the Democratic party to lose sight of the fundamental simplicity of this issue is for the whole party to become a congregation of "yes, but—" fellows.

If the Democratic party knows its century as it has helped to make it, it cannot abandon its hitherto confident and explicit belief that strong and efficient government is the foundation of twentieth-century democracy: its emblem as well as its resource, the very ground and title of its legitimacy. When democracy was in disarray and retreat in 1933, it was Roosevelt who—in the face of Mussolini, in the face of Hitler, in the face of Stalin—demonstrated the ability of democracies *to govern,* to govern not least in a crisis, and to govern efficiently for the purpose of succouring their people in need, without having to keep them in order with storm troopers.

As the Democratic party seemed for a time in 1976 to slip and slide into its preposterous posture of running "against Washington," it needed to remind itself that too many of the "liberties" which are today being claimed from what is pejoratively called big government are in fact privileges only for today's barons and those who are in fee to them. We have all been taught that Magna Carta was—and is—one of the foundations of Anglo-Saxon liberty; and, yes, it was and is. But there was something to be said for King John, even though he was a "bad king"; and Anglo-Saxon liberties were in fact wrought as much by a strong monarchy—a strong central government—as by the tabulation of the selfish privileges which the barons managed to extract for themselves at Runnymede. When the private power of the barons—of the great corporations—is necessarily as great as it is in modern society, it must be the view of what Roosevelt called "the liberal party," meaning by that the Democratic party in this century, that it can be checked only by a dynamic assertion of the public power in its political forms.

The Democratic party was not in the end seduced by George Wallace, but it was tempted by him. Yet it should have known that when Wallace attacks big corporations *and* big unions *and* big government with equal vehemence, there can be only one winner: the corporations. In the end, not only our culture but our politics would be brought to us by "a grant from Mobil Oil." By such a grant even the presidential debates might be shown to the helots.

The real importance of Jimmy Carter's campaign in 1976 was neither in his rhetoric, although that contained clues that were too often overlooked, nor in the substance of his proposals, for the specific proposals of a candidate who has not yet been the president are of questionable value; it was in the demonstration, from the moment that he became visible as a candidate, that his political character was that of a man who had the capacity to govern strongly. That he intended to use the government: It was this that came through, it was this in the end that rescued him from his mistakes, and it was this that set him firmly in the tradition of his own party in this age; and it is to this that he must hold and be held in office.

But that political character had to be joined to a party that felt itself to be itself, and was recognizable to the electors as such. The re-creation of that party in its own image was essentially the work of one man. With all his follies—and he was one of the most foolish of candidates—with all his arrogance—and few men who have sought to capture their party and then to win an election with it, have been so arrogant—George McGovern mapped the furture course of the Democratic party; and it should not be a surprise that he did it by putting it back on course.

It might be said of him, as the *New Republic* said of Al Smith almost fifty years earlier, that the party needed to lose with him rather than win with anyone else. The McGovern reforms were often perverse; their perversity was probably necessary to ensure that a later truth could be extracted. The quota representation of minorities within the party's structure was an absurdity; the emblem of the quotes was probably necessary to ensure that the minorities would be included. The reward came in the midterm election in 1974, as the white working class, and the blacks, and the Catholics, and the farmers, and the women, and the Chicanos, gave the Democratic party commanding majorities in both the Senate and the House of Representatives, and among the governors in the states: majorities which were in fact generally to be increased in 1976, while a president was also added.

In an interesting observation which he made after the 1976 election, Kevin Phillips, the master strategist of "The Emerging Republican Majority" a few years before, said that the New Deal coalition had "command a majority of the country's white voters in all four post-1932 elections," but that in the eight elections since 1948 the Democratic party had won a majority of the white vote only once, in 1964. He then added: "And the operating reality here is very simple—no coalition that lacks the support of the white majority can have the strength or impact that the New Deal coalition had." It is a shrewd point, but he mistakes its meaning.

A majority of the white voters would only be necessary to have the same strength and impact as the New Deal coalition if the nonwhites and others had not been brought, not only into the political system as such, but into the nation. Implicit in Phillips's observation is that the nation is white in the sense that it was in the 1930s and the 1940s, and that the nonwhites are in some sense still apart from it, residents in the nation but semidetached.

The whole meaning of the entry of the nonwhites into his own country in the past half century is almost brushed aside: Unless there is a majority of *white* voters— merely *American* voters will not do—the impact and strength of a coalition must be denied. Yet it was just such an American coalition, founded on America as it had become by the 1970s, that the McGovern reforms began to put together. For what Phillips overlooks is that another "minority" had been found by the Democratic party within the whites themselves. A new breed of women had been invited to come in 1972, and in 1976 they had stayed.

But above all what the conception of a white majority does not take into account is the fact that from as early as 1932, under the leadership of Roosevelt and the initial shrewdness of Jim Farley, the Democratic party recognized that it needed the black vote. So it brought the blacks into the electoral system, and in doing so it brought them into the nation, which is exactly how democracy is intended to work: to compel attention to those who need attention.

Far more than John Kennedy, although his contribution cannot be altogether neglected, it was Lyndon Johnson who, in the words of Herbert Parmet, "reaffirmed the Democratic Party as the agency of reform." When he launched his attack on poverty, he "did not know whether he would pass a single law or appropriate a single dollar. But one thing I did know: When we got through, no one in this country would be able to ignore the poverty in our midst." Of the poor themselves he said: "They lived in the hollows of Appalachia and the hill country of central Texas, in swamp-and-desert, in canebrake and forest, and in the crumbling slums of every American city and every state. They were black and they were white, of every religious background and national origin, and they were 35 million strong."

Down to the enumeration of their numbers—which is also of course an enumeration of potential votes—that is the voice of the Democratic party carried across half a century, the serenade to which at last it always returns. As the public opinion surveys after the 1976 election showed, if the poor had voted in proportion to their numbers, as they never do, Carter's majority would have been larger; and it must be a primary electoral and so political objective of his administration to bring more of them to the polls in 1980 as Roosevelt did in 1936, and so more of them into the heritage of their country.

But there is more—there is much more—to it than that. If it is to survive not only to win elections but to govern well, the Democratic party has to rediscover its belief that the white majority, in what are lumped together as "the suburbs," can be stirred by the humanitarian impulse of their own country, as they once were for the poor immigrants; that liberalism is not to them necessarily dead; that they can be persuaded to believe, as Lyndon Johnson believed, that "at the heart of it, I thought of the Great Society as an extension of the Bill of Rights."

The Party on the Back of Its President

WHATEVER MAY BE THE immediate or the eventual judgment on Jimmy Carter in office, it is already clear that the main theses of this book—that one of the things that most matters is the relationship between a president and his party, and the need for that party to have a strong public philosophy with which it acts on him—are going to be as crucially significant as ever. There is sufficient evidence in his first months in office to suggest again that a president without such a party on his back, even while he stands on its shoulders, may float too freely in space.

During the election in 1976, we were told on every side that the American liberal is no more; that none of the issues with which he is concerned any longer have much appeal to the public; and that even the liberal candidates, such as Morris Udall, did not want to have the label strung round their necks, and would prefer instead to be known as progressives. But there is something implausible in these obituary notices. Great political movements—ideas, ideologies, if one wishes to call them that—simply do not die like that. In fact, we need to realize that the great "-isms" of the modern age—not the vile and shabby "-isms" like Nazism—have a genuine life of their own.

231

They survive because they represent realities, ways in which people perceive the world around them. "Conservatism" and "liberalism," "socialism" and "communism," may change from time to time, and lose their footing; but they do not go away. They are all ways of seeing the actual world.

We have only to think what the world would be like if liberalism were no longer a force to realize that without the liberals we would have lost one hold on the reality of our times. A man such as Udall represents something that will not die, and that we would not like to die; if one searches one's vocabulary, and comes up with words like *decency* and *humor,* then those are also realities. There are people who are witnesses to the ways in which we can know ourselves, including the best in us; and Udall is one of them.

Let us imagine the kind of liberal of whom we are speaking, and give them names, Ruth and David. They are not childless. On the contrary, they seem to have been determined to maintain the reproduction rate of the species, and therefore not to have been satisfied with the two-child family. Moreover, since they believe that a family should be a democracy—like the direct democracy of the Greek city-states in which every citizen participates—they have had enough children to populate it with enough citizens. The conservative is not, as is often thought, the true defender of the family; it is Ruth and David who maintain it in a world unfriendly to it.

The intensity of their attachment to the family can sometimes be irritating. The little citizens of the little city-state are always being noticed and counted, asked their opinions and encouraged to vote. But Ruth and David are intense, not only in their care for their children but in their celebration of their ancestors. They are the real keepers of photograph albums. It is they who tell how their mothers baked a cake, and their fathers read Emerson to them at night; and who want to bake a cake their mothers baked, and read Emerson aloud to their children as their fathers read. They will bridge the generation gap. Like the Greek city-state itself, the American liberal family is one of the most consciously controlled environments that can be imagined.

With every nod to permissiveness, with every inquiry to

the infant about whether it wants to be breast-fed—and it *will* be breast-fed, like it or not—and when—and it *will* be every four hours, like it or not—with every vote taken to decide when the children may first enjoy sex—and they *will* enjoy it, like it or not—the family is strongly led and directed, and as strongly maintained.

But this in recent years has been one of the problems of Ruth and David, or the American liberal. They will be out on the streets at the drop of a hat, to assert the right of everyone else to "do their own thing," but they themselves are intensely concerned to pass on the values of their parents, and of their grandparents. It is they—and not those who are said to be conservative—who know exactly the day on which their grandparents first landed in New York. Ruth and David want to rear other Ruths and Davids, and to pass on values and attitudes that were passed on to them. In their own lives, they are preservers and guardians of values. Yet again and again, in their public concerns, they seem to be tolerant of a social environment that must erode those values.

Just as few people are more quintessentially the American liberal than George McGovern, so few are more quintessentially the representatives of traditional values than he. Yet in the popular mind in 1972—and not without some justice—the campaign of George McGovern was associated with social attitudes that seemed only to be destructive of those values. This geological fault in the liberal is one of the keys to his and her present ineffectiveness. Ruth and David wish their own children to be well educated; but they support *for others* every simpleminded "experimental" program that would reduce education to little more than play-therapy. They do not like to see their own children stoned; but they support *for others* a permissiveness that can reduce a child to inertia and fecklessness. They do not care for pornography; but they support *for others* the right to publish any obscenity. And so on, through the whole gamut of their attitudes.

There is a profound elitism in this: Let the traditional values of everyone else go to pot—almost literally—but they will maintain the benefits of those traditional values for themselves and their children. This is the fault: The slippage of the liberal. One could look at Morris Udall in 1976, as at George McGovern four years earlier, and see in him a man who in all his bearing represents the most traditional values, and yet whose public positions too often leave ordinary people wondering if he would defend those values *for them*. This is one reason why on the social issues lying behind the more directly political issues, the American liberal has made himself more vulnerable and less influential than ever before.

The fact that the American liberal is and sees himself as the guardian of the traditional values of the country, cannot be overestimated. As has been argued throughout this book, Ruth and David are more a part of what America has been made since the mass immigration in this century than any conservative. No one thinks of the period since the Second World War, when the Republican party has twice occupied the White House for the length of two full terms, as Republican years. We naturally think of them as Democratic years because it is the Democrats who have borne the two great ordeals of America in that time—the civil rights movement and the Vietnam War—and whatever the mistakes that in hindsight may be seen to have been made, it has been the Democratic party that has made them, that has endured the pain and bears the scars, and that therefore most surely knows its country.

Parties have histories and folklores, they have characters; and the liberals are not going to recover the certainty of their voice in their own party, and therefore the certainty of the party's voice in the country, unless they bring the values they strive to preserve in their own lives into a clearer relationship with those that they seem to support in their public stances. They need to be much more aware of the meaning of their guardianship, much more attentive to where they have come from, even if it seems that they have come so far.

But let us look at the attitudes of Ruth and David from another angle. They all but ceased to think of public issues in economic terms, hence their preoccupation with the social questions, with the qualitative instead of the quantitative issues, as Arthur Schlesinger put it so long ago. They fritter too much in the margins, and the great economic questions go by default. They do not know how to steel their president against the corporations or, for that matter, against Arthur Burns; and are left to complain that he is more conservative than they expected, when it is their own conservatism that he reflects.

Tucked away on Ruth's and David's shelves will be found the liberal literature of the 1930s and the 1940s in which social questions were confronted first as economic questions. Now they read John Kenneth Galbraith—or rather they have read some of the versions of his own gospel—and all they seem to get out of him is that somehow it is wrong to consume, and certainly that it is wrong to consume what is impure. This seems to have become all that concerns them, and that does not make a program for a party.

David and Ruth seem unable to come to grips with the economic system as a whole, a system which by distributing goods to satisfied consumers has found the way of ensuring that there will be no demand for a genuine redistribution of power. The social questions with which Ruth and David are today so preoccupied are not—and cannot be made into—genuine political questions unless they are first identified as economic questions; and that is exactly what none of the liberal standard-bearers in recent years— Adlai Stevenson and George McGovern and Morris Udall will do, to say nothing of Eugene McCarthy, whom it is hard to identify as a liberal. Missing from the influences on a Democratic president today is the pressure of a strong and coherent body of liberal opinion within the party itself that will force him to try to do more than merely make the economic system work a little more satisfactorily for a slightly greater number of people.

The New Deal was not merely a series of brilliant improvisations. Those improvisations were locked into the permanent structure of the country in part because there was a strong liberal critique within the Democratic party that was based on an intellectually adventurous examination of the economic system in the first half of the twentieth century. It may be said that the examination did not go deep enough, nor the New Deal far enough. But within the context of the times and the circumstances, permanent gains were made within those fields in which the Democratic party is bound to act if it is to recover the sense of its own tradition in this century and keep its support.

What must concern the liberal, and therefore the Democratic party, and therefore a Democratic president, is that the economic realm has for more than a generation now displaced the political realm. As has been argued here, it has been the virtue of the Democrats in this century that they have believed in politics; they must therefore believe in another emphatic assertion of the political power over the economic power; and there is ample evidence that when a Democratic president is not subject to intense pressure from the liberal left within his own party he will be weak or only intermittent in his assertion of the political power and leave the economic realm safe for those who dominate it.

Why does a Democratic president no longer speak the kind of language that Franklin Roosevelt used when he spoke of "economic royalists"? There are economic barons in the United States who are in a position to usurp the central power of the state, and sometimes do, whose own power is so interlocked with that of government that at times it almost seems to be true that the system has become one of socialism for the rich—it is they who are always buoyed by subsidies—and capitalism for the poor—it is they who must swim or sink. This is not a situation the Democrats can tolerate for long, or they will again and again send back to the White House a president they can only nag to be bolder. As was said at the beginning, in 1976 it was not so much a case of a presidential candidate not having a coherent policy, but a case of a party that did not know what it wanted its candidate to do if elected; and the results will be there to be seen, and may already be visible.